Summertime

Photograph, glass globe, circa 1873. S. R. Stoddard, master photographer and author, spent his summer plying his trade around Lake George and upper New York State during the 1870s. The reflected image shows Mr. Stoddard and his stereo camera on the front lawn of the Fort William Henry Hotel.

Summertime

Photographs of Americans at Play 1850-1900

Floyd and Marion Rinhart

Clarkson N. Potter, Inc./Publishers

DISTRIBUTED BY CROWN PUBLISHERS, INC., NEW YORK

Books by Floyd and Marion Rinhart

American Daguerrean Art
American Miniature Case Art
America's Affluent Age
America's Centennial Celebration: Philadelphia, 1876

Picture Credits

The illustrations reproduced in this book were supplied by courtesy of the following individuals and institutions:

George Bolster, 145–146.
Josephine Cobb, 11, 137(b).
Dr. & Mrs. N. Dinhofer, 63(b), 77(b), 97(b), 165(b), 166(a), 179(b).
N. Sherrill Foster, 78(a), 81, 83, 86.
Emerick Hanzl, 114.
Historical Society of Saratoga Springs, N.Y., 147, 148(a), 149(a).
Carlton Kelsey, 78–79.
Museum of the City of New York, 14–15, 66, 67, 70, 75.
Nantucket Historical Association, 101, 102(a).
New-York Historical Society, 9, 61(b), 64–65, 153.
New-York Historical Society, Bella C. Landauer Collection, 140(b).
George H. Moss, Jr., 22, 34–35, 38, 40, 42, 43, 50, 53, 55, 56, 58, 59, 60, 61(a), 62, 63(a), 91(a).
George R. Rinhart, 17(a), 18, 20(b), 23(b), 24(b), 25, 27(a), 28–29, 42–43(b), 44, 45, 46, 47, 72(b),
    73, 76, 77(a), 88, 94, 95, 97, 98, 99(a), 104, 106, 108, 109, 110, 111, 112, 115, 132, 133, 136(b),
    137(a&b), 138, 141, 157, 158, 159 (a&b), 160, 162, 163, 164, 165(a), 166(b), 167, 168, 169, 172(b),
    173, 178, 183, 184, 185, 186, 187.
Rockwood Museum, 36(a), 37.
Yale University Library, Gertrude Stein Collection, 107(a&b).
Authors' Collection, 2, 6, 10, 12, 13, 17(b&c), 20(a,c,&d), 21, 22, 23(a), 27(b), 32, 36(b), 41, 48, 49,
    57, 66(b), 72(a), 74(b), 80, 82(a), 84, 86–87, 89, 90, 91(b), 99(b), 100, 102(b), 105, 107, 113, 114,
    116, 117, 118, 119, 120–121, 123, 124, 125, 126, 127, 130, 136, 138, 139, 140, 142–143, 150, 152,
    155, 167, 170, 171, 172(a), 174, 175, 176–177, 180, 181, 182.

Editorial direction by Carol Southern
Production supervision by Michael Fragnito
Design by Ed Sneider and Kathy Jungjohann
Composition by Publishers Phototype, Inc.
Printing and binding by Halliday Lithograph Corporation

Published simultaneously in Canada by General Publishing Company Limited

First edition

Printed in the United States of America

Designed by Ed Schneider and Kathy Jungjohann

Library of Congress Cataloging in Publication Data
Rinhart, Floyd.
    Summertime.

    Bibliography: p.
    Includes index.
    1. Atlantic States—Description and travel. 2. Summer resorts—Atlantic States.
I. Rinhart, Marion, joint author. II. Title.
F106.R67   1977   974   76-26501
ISBN 0-517-52492-9

Contents

The bather, a tintype, circa 1879.

Acknowledgments

This book would not have been possible without the help of our son George R. Rinhart, New York City, collector and dealer in rare photographics and president of the long-established firm of Underwood and Underwood, Inc.

Other collectors, institutions, librarians, and directors of historical societies who have provided photographs, pictorial material, or have kindly helped in research for this book are as follows: George Bolster, Saratoga Springs, N.Y.; Josephine Cobb, Cape Elizabeth, Maine; Dr. and Mrs. Norman Dinhofer, Brooklyn, N.Y.; N. Sherrill Foster, East Hampton, N.Y.; Emerick Hanzl, Clifton, N.J.; Susan Leslie, Historical Society of Saratoga Springs, N.Y.; Carleton Kelsey, Amagansett, N.Y.; Charles T. Lyle, Monmouth County Historical Association, Freehold, N.J.; Maine Historical Society, Portland, Maine; George H. Moss, Jr., Rumson, N.J.; Esther Brumberg, Museum of the City of New York, N.Y.; Leroy H. True, Nantucket Historical Association, Nantucket, Mass.; New-York Historical Society, New York, N.Y.; New York State Library, Albany, N.Y.; Ohio State University, Columbus, O.; Rockwood, The Shipley-Bringhurst-Hargraves Museum, Wilmington, Del.; Mildred Kaliski, Cape May Courthouse Library, Cape May, N.J.; Donald Gallup, Yale University Library, New Haven, Conn.

Introduction

Like a bombshell, the news from Paris of Louis J. M. Daguerre's discovery exploded on the Western world in August of 1839. The invention, named the daguerreotype in his honor, was a photograph on a thin copper plate coated with silver. For the first time people could see a small replica of an image with all the exactness and proportion reproduced from nature and, as one artist exclaimed, "From today painting is dead."

While the theory of "photogenic drawings" or "sun paintings," as photography was then called, was not new in 1839, it was Daguerre's beautiful and permanently fixed images that excited the imagination. The Englishman William H. F. Talbot succeeded in producing a paper negative in 1835 and by 1839 a paper print. The Daguerre and Talbot discoveries would be the foundation for later improved forms of photography.

The new art came to America in September 1839, when booklets outlining Daguerre's process reached New York aboard the British *Queen.* At first only scenes were made because of the long exposure time required. Men of science like Samuel F. B. Morse and Dr. John W. Draper were determined to improve Daguerre's basic process so that portraits of people could be taken. Time exposure by the fall of 1840 had been cut from minutes to seconds, and by 1841, as a result of pioneering experiments, rooftop and open-sunlight photographs gave way to the indoor portrait using skylights as a source of light.

In America the daguerreotype quickly became a truly native art and reached the greatest heights in the late 1840s during an era of great scientific achievement. From its very beginnings in March 1840, when the first commercial portrait gallery in the world was established, Americans flocked to have their likenesses taken even though the venture into the unknown of a Daguerrean gallery with its mysterious equipment was a fearsome adventure! *Godey's Lady's Book*

Photographer with subjects, Central Park, New York City, circa 1885. Central Park made an ideal setting for the many amateurs who turned to photography as a hobby in the 1880s.

(1849) noted: "In our great cities, a Daguerreotypist is to be found in almost every square ... A few years ago it was not every man who could afford a likeness of himself, his wife or his children ... now it is hard to find the man who has not gone through the 'operator's hands' from once to a half-a-dozen times, or has not the shadowy faces of his wife and children done up in purple morocco and velvet, together or singly, among his household treasures."

The mirrorlike daguerreotype gradually gave way to other photographic processes in the 1850s. The first to challenge the daguerreotype was the ambrotype, a photograph on glass that became popular in 1854. In 1856 a photograph on thin sheet iron, later called a tintype, was introduced. Meanwhile paper photography was being improved. Talbot's negatives on paper

A stereo view card. "Around the piano," circa 1858.

had been mostly replaced by glass negatives. Sensitizing materials and photographic papers were greatly improved and became easier to produce. By the close of the 1850 decade, the advantage of many paper prints from a single negative attracted professional and amateur photographers and hastened the decline of the ambrotype and the daguerreotype. Only the cheap and quickly produced tintype remained as a competitor!

Many reproductions from stereo view cards have been used throughout this book. The history of stereographic photography closely paralleled the development of other styles of photography. Some readers will recall childhood memories, looking through grandfather's old stereo viewer at amusing or instructive scenes and people—a counterpart to a modern-day TV program.

Popular fancy was caught up by the stereoscope in America following the Crystal Palace Exhibition of 1851, London, when the Brewster stereoscope was shown for the first time to the public. The idea had originated back in 1838 when Sir Charles Wheatstone, discoverer of the principle, made an instrument by which binocular pictures were made to combine through the use of mirrors. Sir David Brewster invented in 1849 a lens-stereoscope in which a series of stereoscopic pictures could be viewed in rapid succession.

John F. Mascher, a Philadelphian, patented a daguerreotype case stereoscope in 1853 in which two daguerreotypes placed in the case could be viewed (in three-dimensional effect) through a flap in which had been fitted two ordinary magnifying glasses. Soon other larger table model stereoscopes were invented by Americans for stereoscopic viewing of daguerreotypes, ambrotypes, and by the mid-1850s paper stereo prints mounted on cardboard.

Stereo views did not reach great popularity until the late 1850s when Oliver Wendell Holmes publicized them in the *Atlantic Monthly* and in 1859 invented a small hand

Waterfalls, a paper print, circa 1867.

stereo-viewer. By 1860 the *Scientific American* remarked on stereo cards and the viewers: "Its cost is so little that we can calculate on its penetrating to the homes of the humblest man."

To make stereoscopic views a special camera with two lenses was used, although some veterans kept to the old way of separating two cameras rather widely to create a stereoscopic effect. When prints were made from the stereoscopic negative, they were cut in two, and they were then trimmed to desired shape whether square, oval, or with an arch at top. The print to the right was mounted on cardboard on the left side and the left-hand print was mounted on the right side of the card. When viewed through twin magnifying glasses of a stereo viewer, the two photographs mounted on one card, side by side, blended into a single three-dimensional picture quite startling in its realism.

The professional photographer had a horse-drawn wagon to carry his darkroom tent and supplies when traveling. His glass plates had to be coated with sensitized collodion in darkness. After he took a picture he quickly returned to the tent to develop his negative and to prepare another plate if other views were to be taken. Later, the prepared dry plates did away with much of the heavy field equipment.

After the Civil War, many photographers followed the old tradition, roaming about the country and seaside in the summertime, and by following the crowds to resorts they often combined business with pleasure. Some set up shanties or rented space to practice tintyping. Others brought their double-view stereo cameras and pitched their tents near a large hotel—often in competition with the local photographers.

Robert Newell, of Philadelphia, was one of the city photographers who traveled to the seaside during the summer to photograph the fashionables. In early July of 1866 Newell set off for Cape May with a dark tent wagon to carry his photographic equipment. His first problem on reaching the resort was to secure a room for printing and mounting purposes, although his dark tent would serve well for preparing and developing his negatives. His tent wagon became a portable studio on the beach. It had a large muslin-type awning to shade the patrons from the glare of sun and sand while he manipulated his camera. The fashionable bathing hours were from 11 A.M. to 1 P.M. Mr. Newell said, "Every shot must be a hit—no time for mistakes."

On rainy days at Cape May, according to the New York *Times* (1875), there were two methods of diversion—to sit in the hotel hall and listen to the band play "Mulligan Guards" or to lounge on the piazza and be photographed "en bloc." In the latter case, the photographer, after a little speech, aimed his camera from a balcony. In his friendly way he suggested changes in position, to a gentleman in the front with a child on

Field photographer, circa 1871.

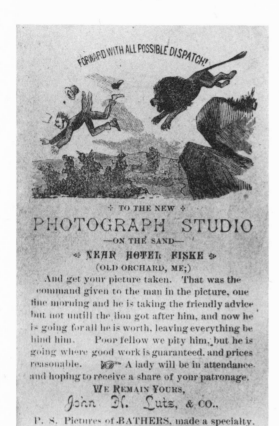

"You divine little creature, are you our new cook?" circa 1900.

his knee or to a lady head averted as though looking at someone. The photographer's manner was serious despite titters from the audience. The crowd soon assumed the stony aspect believed appropriate for the occasion, with all expression gone. "Remain like that," yells the artist. He rushes from the balcony, returns with a slide, fidgets with his camera, removes the black cloth, gazes anxiously at his victims while he counts to thirty. The final announcement—"That will do, ladies and gentlemen." The next day the photographer appeared at the hotel to sell the portraits at fifty cents each.

For photographers living near lake or river resorts, the natural thing to do was to pack a camera and equipment and enjoy a sailing trip. One such photographer was S. R. Stoddard of Glens Falls, New York. Some of his views of Lake George are reproduced in this book. Stoddard had a sailboat called the *Wanderer*. He wandered all over Lake George taking views and making money selling them to the various hotels, which in turn sold photographs along with cigars to their patrons. On the sail of Stoddard's boat was a picture that he called his coat of arms—Stoddard astride a camera in pursuit of wealth, represented by a bulging moneybag with wings.

Summer photographers were also commissioned by hotel owners and owners of summer homes to take views, and fees were rather good, especially if on assignment.

The photographs reproduced in this volume were originally taken by nineteenth-century professional photographers. Some are studio portraits and others were photographed by itinerants. Most of the scenic views and genre subjects were reproduced from stereo view cards. A few tintypes are represented and a sprinkling of carte de visite and cabinet cards are used to show typical portraits of the Victorian age. This style of photograph is very often identified by studio accessories or painted backgrounds. Also included are reproductions from large paper photographs of scenic views, which were pasted in albums or mounted on cardboard. Many of the photographs reproduced are rare and can be found only in specialized collections.

Some of the early action scenes, where people or moving objects are represented, appear rather fuzzy because of slow-acting photographic materials or poorly prepared collodion and developers. Long exposure shots are often sharp and beautiful. Other unusual views have faded and have been difficult to reproduce.

The reader of this book may be startled to find, in the midst of Victorian propriety, comic genre scenes, some a bit naughty. The comic view scenes, depicting domestic strife or other amusing episodes, were posed by studio models. They were usually produced in quantity and in a series to provide a touch of comedy for stereoscope viewers.

"They are sound asleep," 1899.

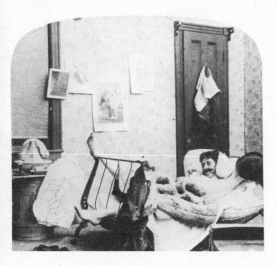

"Country Accommodations," 1897.

"In the Wrong Room," 1897.

In the days before the picture postcard, the stereo photographer sought to capture attractive views of buildings, landscapes, local events, and people at work or play, which he would then sell, often in a series, to the summer tourists as vacation keepsakes. Stereo views could also be bought locally from stationery, book, and department stores, or they could be ordered from catalogs.

The years from 1860 to 1880 were ones of great activity for the small independent photographer who took, mounted, and published his own stereo cards, generally with his name imprinted. A number of successful photographers during the period, like the Kilburn brothers of New Hampshire and William Chase of Baltimore, devoted their full time to photographing and publishing stereo view cards. Also, there were large photographic supply houses, like E. & H. T. Anthony of New York, that maintained separate departments for producing stereo views. These establishments usually employed their own staff photographers or bought offerings from photographers in various locations about the country.

By the end of the century the sale of stereo views had become a big business, often slanted toward education in the home. New names, like Keystone and Underwood & Underwood, became the byword for massive production.

After going over thousands of old photographs taken in the post Civil War years up to 1900, we concluded that most modern historians had missed a vital segment of American social history—summer life at the resorts. The graphic picture presented by the photographs bears little relation to the dreary years depicted by the historians who relied mostly on lithographs and cartoons of a sensational nature to show American life in that era.

To help the reader enter into the spirit of the age, we have dated, as accurately as possible, all of the photographic reproductions. When reproducing from stereo view cards, we have taken the clearest and best of the two views represented on the card. Because of the widespread interest in the history of photography, we have included an appendix, which will provide additional information on each photograph used. Text has been taken primarily from periodicals and guide books of the period. Though quotes are sometimes attributed, more often they are not in order to keep a readable flow; a complete bibliography is given at the end of the book.

—*Floyd and Marion Rinhart*
1978

*The staff of the music publisher M. Witmark & Sons leaving for an excursion up
the Hudson to Newburgh.*

Summer Exodus

Early Days

The fashion of summering away from home did not begin early in America. Colonial Americans found nowhere as healthy or enjoyable as home when cities were small and water still pure. Very few country seats existed and these were close enough to the cities to be visited on foot. However, as the population grew and cities expanded, the wealthy began visiting nearby mineral springs to take the cure.

In the early days only robust and adventuresome men journeyed by wagon to the seashore or other distant watering places. Improvements in roads, carriages, and especially steamboats soon brought out a full complement of ladies, which according to one historian gave an air of gaiety and good manners to the steamboats, stagecoaches, and inns.

By the 1820s many resorts had become rendezvous for high society, and places like Saratoga, Ballston, and Nahant were crowded during the summer months.

By the 1830s, the crotchety old stagecoach developed into a link for steamboat and railroad lines. The colorful side-wheeler steamboats had become longer and faster, and railroads began spreading their spiderlike network about eastern America. The East attracted people from all areas of the country. Resorts flourished from Cape May to Bar Harbor and from the Thousand Islands to Niagara. The tradition of summering away from home was established.

Nathaniel P. Willis, a discerning commentator on American life, gave the flavor of the time when he wrote in 1840 about the popular Hudson River voyage to Albany. "All passengers," he said, "arrived at the narrow pier just before departure time—seven hundred men, ladies, and children, besides lapdogs, crammed baskets, uncut novels, and baggage." When the travelers were all settled, the plank was drawn in, the wheels began to churn, the bell rang, and the voyage began. An hour out of New York, young ladies began to read their novels and old gentlemen their newspapers. By then the captain had received his fares, locked them up in his office, and was off for a smoke with the engineer.

The English had long been visitors to the States, but Americans were also traveling abroad in large numbers in the 1840s and 1850s, and wherever they went they proudly displayed their wealth. Perhaps the cutting criticisms about American society from the pens of Mrs. Trollope, Harriet Martineau, and Charles Dickens goaded the American tourist to "lord it over" the British.

One American traveling about Europe in 1847 said that none of the sea-bathing places compared with the natural beauty of Cape May or Long Branch. Further, he said that England's Brighton was spoiled by the "dampness of English society."

However, American resorts had one great drawback; they could not keep up with the crowds brought in by the new fast trains and steamboats, and more new hotels and boardinghouses had to be built with improved service. There was no stopping the restless American— the age of summering had come into its own.

Iron Bridge, Portage, first test train, July 31, 1875. The Erie Railroad's bridge over the Genesee Falls, said by some to be the largest wooden bridge in the world, was destroyed by fire on May 6, 1875. Work on a new iron bridge was started on June 1, 1875. The first test train—six of the Erie's largest locomotives and tenders loaded with coal and water—crossed the iron bridge just two months later.

16

"The New Woman," 1897. The "new woman," clad in knickers, astride a bicycle, was not welcome at every resort. The dowagers of Cape May gathered forces in an anti-bicycle club.

Portrait of young lady, Thompson's Hotel, Lake Mahopac, New York, circa 1869. The American girl was the darling of any resort, sought after by "fast young men." English visitors marveled at her resourcefulness and freedom, that she could go anywhere without a chaperone—unthinkable in Europe!

A gentleman in bathing dress, circa 1888.

English Viewpoint

From Benjamin Franklin's time, foreign travelers coming to America agreed on one thing—that Americans as a whole were quite barbaric, excepting perhaps Bostonians, the most English and so most hospitable and cultured.

Two English visitors while visiting the States in 1869 compared the pace of American life with their homeland: " 'Yankee Doodle' is much faster than 'God Save the Queen.' " They found American watering places busy, contrasting sharply with the quiet life at English resorts where the weary sought peace and quiet to recuperate from life's daily toil. "At American watering-places . . . all is life and activity; the houses (commonly called 'cottages,' in the pride of humility) are elegantly furnished, and are replete with every comfort and luxury. Small children are kept in the background. . . ."

Magnesia Spring, Sharon Springs, New York, circa 1867.

Summer people, the Englishmen said, devoted themselves to sea bathing, croquet, driving, sailing, walking, flirting, and partygoing. They recalled crowded afternoon balls at summer resorts lasting from 3:00 P.M. until 8:00 P.M. with time out for supper at five o'clock. Suppers were always taken standing—"a great scramble among the men round the tables—in short, in their eagerness to get refreshments for their partners, such scenes are sometimes witnessed as are disgraceful to any civilized society." Fruits at these buffet suppers were varied and fine and the food similar to England's own. Sweet dishes were abundant at all ball suppers and "a very popular but indigestible compound, known as 'chicken salad,' is ever present . . . the most common wine at supper is champagne."

The two Englishmen noted that American businessmen worked so hard they hardly knew how to relax and enjoy a holiday—they seemed content to slave away in business so their families could summer at fashionable resorts.

On the moral tone of Americans, the Englishmen commented: "The morality of American society generally appears to be much more stern than that of the English. A man who transgresses the bounds of decorum in the United States is looked on as a black sheep, to be avoided by all respectable people. . . . The average American is better dressed than the Englishman . . . nor does he care to show his pride through the holes of his coat, as certain great English peers are commonly reported to do. . . . Fortunately, tobacco-chewing is gradually decreasing . . . and is never seen among gentlemen of the best society."

The English marveled that the American girl could go anywhere without a chaperone: "Mothers place so much confidence in their daughters that they allow them not only to walk and drive alone with gentlemen but even to correspond with them, their letters not being under the maternal supervision . . . nowhere, even in Paris, will one see such magnificent toilettes as are displayed at the balls and watering-places . . . The average American girl has undoubtedly prettier features than the average English girl . . . [but] it is said their good looks soon fade." Although they were not considered to be as accomplished in music and foreign languages as their English counterparts, they dressed well and had grace, beauty, and lively manners.

Later in the century other reports floated in concerning the American girl. Oscar Wilde described her as "the most fascinating little despot in the world; an oasis of picturesque unreasonableness in a dreadful desert of common sense." Another description called her "champagny, glittering, foamy, bubbly, sweet, dry, tart, in a word fizzy!" Whatever the American girl's charm or fault, the English visitor found her fascinating and she was the big attraction at the summer resorts.

19

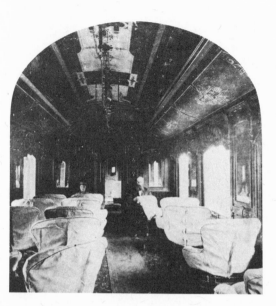

Pullman drawing-room car, circa 1878.

Frankenstein Trestle and train, P. & O. Railroad, Crawford Notch, White Mountains of New Hampshire, circa 1881. One story a traveler heard was that not far from the Frankenstein Trestle, a hunter, many years before, had "found two immense ledges, so overlaid with pure diamonds that their intense light blinded him. He carried out such bits as could be broken away, and sold them at a great price; but neither he nor the adventure seekers who followed his track could ever find the treasure again." The Frankenstein Trestle was 500 feet long and rose 80 feet from the bottom of the ravine.

Dinner on the railroad, circa 1878.

"Railroad Scene," Little Falls, 1838.

How They Traveled

If the elaborate railroad and steamboat brochures of the time are to be believed, the American tourist was as pampered as the blue bloods of Europe. Luxury and comfort pervaded train and boat interiors featuring fine woods, gilt, and elegance. Trains and boats, faster every year, satisfied the American passion for speed.

Once a resort had been decided upon, the ticket agent took over and a legion of helpers stood ready to advise, often subtly guiding the prospective traveler to consider one of the railroad's own fine resort hotels. If the resort chosen were distant, the agent helped with a travel itinerary which included stopovers, transfers, boat and stage connections, all pinpointed with exactness. All tickets were good for one month or longer, and it saved time and frustration to have tickets in hand before departure time. The railroad system of baggage checking was excellent. One hundred fifty pounds were allowed.

A seasoned traveler saved the annoyance of shifting packages and luggage about by taking advantage of the many express companies found at every steamer and railroad station. Luggage could be forwarded to any part of the country and delivered to the desired destination, whether a resort hotel or summer home. Having sent his luggage on its way, a city dweller could take a horsecar or other public conveyance to his train or boat, carrying with him only the barest of necessities.

Travelers had to put up with a certain amount of tyranny from railroad conductors who reigned supreme in the cars. During the day, boys came around on the half hour selling papers, books, sweets, apples, and ice water. Usually one of the cars on the train was better than the others and set aside for women or couples. The smoking car was usually inhabited by "tobacco-chewing roughs" and avoided by proper travelers.

The drawing rooms and palace cars were exclusive and higher priced. At one end of the car was a "saloon" furnished with sofas, armchairs, and spittoons; at the other end were lavatories. The palace cars, owned by private concerns, were expensively fitted out and used for sitting by day and sleeping by night. Bed-making began at 9:00 P.M. during dining hours. The upper and lower berths, screened by curtains at bedtime, resembled berths in a ship's cabin. During the night, gentlemen left their boots in the aisle for polishing and the next morning the porter received his usual tip.

The day excursionist and the stay-all-season vacationer occupied a special niche as preferred customers with the railroads and boat lines. Packaged vacation tours and special round-trip rates had come of age. In the early 1850s the Baltimore & Ohio Railroad ran Fourth of July excursion trains to places outside Baltimore. Next came Atlantic City and the railroad brought fun, frolic, and relief to heat-weary Philadelphians. Other railroads joined the parade.

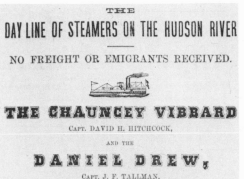

Advertisement for Hudson River Day Line from the Canadian Handbook and Guide, *1868.*

21

Steamer Mt. Washington, *Center Harbor, New Hampshire, circa 1873. The* Mt. Washington *made her debut early in the 1870s to meet the growing demand of the tourist trade on Lake Winnipesaukee.*

When a train or boat reached its destination, hacks and vehicles of all kinds were waiting and ready for the unwary tourists, and all bedlam would break loose. The traveler was immediately surrounded by pushing hack drivers and express agents all loudly crying their merits.

Travel on one of the old steamboats could be most elegant, as evidenced by this excerpt on The Fall River Line from John B. Bachelder's 1875 guidebook:

"On crossing the gang-plank the visitor finds himself on a broad deck, surrounded by richly carved and gilded panelling. The deck itself is composed of alternate strips of yellow pine and black walnut. Large doors in the after bulkhead lead to the ladies' saloons and state-rooms,

22

Saloon, Steamer Drew, *circa 1867. Only the plushest hotels could compete with Daniel Drew's Hudson River steamers. A Wall Street tycoon, Drew knew how to run a first-class steamboat line. The two steamers of the Hudson River Day Line were "probably, without exception, the swiftest steamboats in the world." On a test run, the* Vibbard *made twenty-seven miles an hour.*

which are appropriately divided for the use of ladies travelling alone, and for families with children, the most complete accommodations being provided for all . . . those who desire more luxurious surroundings than are sought by the public at large. . . . These rooms far excel in elegance those of any first class hotel, and in size they are at least equal to the ordinary rooms of seaside houses. . . . The signal gun announces the hour of departure, and these magnificent floating palaces, crowded with human freight, glide into the stream. Martial music, by Hall's Boston Brass Band, enlivens the scene, as the gaily-dressed steamer majestically threads her way through the noble harbor. "

East End Hotel, circa 1873. Expansive "Big" Jim Fisk, the Erie Railroad tycoon, lived in New York's Grand Central Hotel and owned the Grand Opera House. With Jay Gould, he built The Grand Excursion House, which was renamed the East End Hotel after his death. Fisk never missed a chance to steal away to Long Branch and could usually be found surrounded by a bevy of pretty girls. In 1881 a visitor looking for the hotel discovered it had been torn down and only an empty lot remained.

Accommodations: Hotels and Cottages

An American wrote in 1872:

Extravagance and display have almost entirely superseded the old-fashioned economy and comfort. . . . The present generation likes large hotels, and the correspondingly large hotel bills, which imply the desire for unbounded luxuries and the ability to pay for them. Americans, too, more than any other people, are gregarious; and if a man is known by the company he keeps, Americans especially are known by the amount of company they keep, and hence, with perpetual travel and much hotel frequenting, they have and make more acquaintances than any other people in the world. The *table d'hôte* which assembles from one hundred to one thousand persons in a single dining-room, with the accompanying din, as well as dinner, the clatter of cutlery and crockery, and the rush of a regiment of waiters, is an Americanism which is not . . . popular abroad. . . . Nowhere else in the world is the hotel so essentially a "public" house as in the United States; and publicity in its fullest extent in the halls, parlors, reading-rooms, dining-rooms is here preferred to the comparative privacy which is sought in hotels abroad.

In the town of Saratoga, where everything was colossal, the United States Hotel boasted of the largest dining hall in the world.

After the Civil War, much of the new wealth in the country was invested in land and in building hotels for the summer tourist trade. It was playtime now. The Americans who had suffered through the trauma of a great war were looking for the luxury and convenience of big, well-run hotels. Immense hotels were being built at the older seaside resorts like Long Branch and Cape May and along the entire Atlantic coast. Inland resorts, too, like Saratoga and the White Mountains, were replacing old hotels and building new, larger ones.

The summer house, circa 1869. The two-story gingerbread house was a favorite at the resorts—at a cost of about $1,500 to $2,000. An 18-by-40-foot summer cottage would accommodate a parlor, sewing room, and kitchen downstairs, and airy sleeping quarters up above. They had no cellars, no heat, no gas fittings, and no plumbing except for a sink on the rear porch.

"Going with the stream," 1897.

The increasing number of new hotels, boardinghouses, and cottages also lined the pockets of the summer businessmen who catered to the vacation trade. Livery stables, billiard rooms, souvenir shops, ice-cream parlors, photographers all did very well. The biggest money-makers of all were the railroad and steamboat lines, and they in turn reinvested heavily in the resorts.

Up and down the Atlantic coast from Cape May to Bar Harbor big land promotion schemes were in full swing by 1870. Wherever the railroad went, land speculators were sure to follow.

The frame summer cottage built in a modified Gothic or Queen Anne style was all the rage by 1876. "Railroads and steamboats have now become so numerous that all classes, from the humblest mechanic to the wealthy banker, can have their homes in the country. . . . We see studded along the lines of our railroads picturesque and cheerful homes, where the heads of families . . . are recuperating from the deleterious effects of the confinement of city life."

By the century's end the problem of hotel accommodations had been solved—the crowds were there—the prices high. In America's never-ending search for prestige, many of the old-fashioned resorts with modest hotel and cottage accommodations lost out to the newer or more glamorous places.

Dryden Springs Place, Dryden, New York, circa 1874. An elderly man has just been to the fountain for his pitcher of "sulphur" water. The springs, located ten miles from Ithaca, was one of the many New York State springs in the "sulphur" category.

The Spas

"Under what roof shall we find undiluted milk, digestable bread, and . . . homely genuine fare" were some of the questions concerning older people and invalids who hoped to find a summer lodging where they could regain their health. Many felt that the water they drank was as important to their recovery as wholesome food.

The healing properties of medicinal and mineral springwater in eastern America were long known to the Indians. Colonials began visiting nearby springs, and tales were handed down through the generations about their curative powers. Resorts soon grew up around the better-known healing fountains and they became fashionable as well as healthful.

Making the rounds of the various springs, or "spring hopping," became a popular pastime, but the chronic invalid had to choose a spring best suited to his cure. Each had special medicinal properties—some acid water, some borax, others sulfur—and the various springs

Birch-Dale Springs Hotel, circa 1872. A modest hotel for the tourist in search of quiet, and accessible to four separate springs. The pure cold water of the hundreds of springs in the northeast was said to have been proved highly effective in treating "rheumatic, cutaneous, and dyspeptic complaints."

John Allen's camp-meeting tent, circa 1870. Roughing it in tents was nothing new to many Americans. All during the nineteenth century camp meetings drew thousands of the religious to summer retreats for several days of preaching and prayers. Tents could be hired at the camp meeting grounds for as little as $100 to $200 for the season.

were tested and their precise mineral content labelled. Well-known doctors or professors often made statements to the public about the special healing qualities of the springs for particular ailments.

Boardinghouses or small hotels catered to these needs, but more popular were the "water cure" establishments. These "houses" found at the springs were usually directed by doctors who advertised "wholesome food, experienced medical advice, and other facilities," and promised to make the invalid's stay a pleasant and comfortable one. Hot and cold baths of various kinds were featured and spring water, the one most suited to the invalid's needs, was given as part of a prescribed health routine. If a famous celebrity "watered" at a certain establishment the word was soon out and it helped business.

New York State was peppered with springs. Ballston and Saratoga Springs were the first of many resorts famous for their help to invalids, but when Saratoga became very fashionable the invalid clientele often chose less pretentious resorts.

People suffering from hay fever were likely to choose the White Mountains for a summer place, and those who suffered from consumption or other lung ailments also sought the pure air of the mountaintops. Others preferred the sea air and sea bathing as the most beneficial. Whatever their complaint, the invalid had a wide choice of resorts.

Camping Out

Many Americans with big families found the cost of fashionable resorts much too high and the rooms too confining for busy active children, but the very thought of vacationing at a cheap boardinghouse sent shivers up their spines. Thus, a new trend developed in the 1870s, the answer for those who had to watch their money. It was camping out.

Old-time camp meetings began taking on a new look which combined religion and summer pleasure. Methodists led the way by purchasing land in prime vacation areas like Ocean Grove, New Jersey, Martha's Vineyard, and Thousand Islands Park on the St. Lawrence River. Many smaller camp-meeting sites were established in other states including New York, Maine, and Massachusetts. The peak of scheduled religious events came in August and thousands upon thousands attended. Families and friends coming for the season often shared rented tents or lived in combination tent-cottages. The camping out movement with its wholesome good fellowship among Christian families brought about a great new religious revival in the East.

Families and friends began getting together to make plans for summer camping in the mountains, the lake country, or by the sea. One group of about eight families, in 1874, camped together on the shore of a lake, bringing thirteen tents—one to be used as a dining room, a second for the kitchen, and a smaller one for provisions. Each of the family tents contained one or two beds, a washstand, and a bureau (some used a trunk)—each had a rustic parlor which extended from a sheltered wooden platform. Every tent had a fine view of the lake scenery, and hammocks were suspended under nearby trees, for reading or loafing. Women brought along fancywork for the quiet times. On clear days, boating, fishing, and excursions on the lake took first priority. Clothing was light and comfortable and the unhampered children could climb trees and dig in the dirt to their heart's content. Coming along with the party to make life easier were three cooks and two coachmen. A carriage and a light wagon were sent to town every morning for fresh supplies, and milk was bought from a nearby farm where the horses were stabled. At summer's end the vacation was voted a success.

Tents made in three sizes, opening up like umbrellas of striped canvas to hold six to twelve persons, were manufactured by a Boston company. They could be pitched in ten minutes (so they said) and weighed only fifty pounds. Another Boston company sold in 1875 a camp stove with a detachable oven and neatly nested cooking utensils. The stove and fittings weighed only twenty-seven pounds and sold for fifteen dollars.

Even with all the inconveniences of camp life, an interval of getting back to the woods had many followers. A bout with nature was never so tiring as keeping up with the Joneses at a fashionable resort.

Camp Hughes, Hitchen's Pond, Tupper Lake, circa 1879. All kinds of game could be had in the Adirondacks; bear was hunted the year round, except on Sundays, and venison was the hunter's main bill of fare.

Bathing in the surf, Nantucket, 1883.

By the Sea

Cape May

Rumor may have reached the colonials that King George III had taken to sea bathing for his health. In any event, before the Revolutionary War a number of Philadelphians visited the little settlement of Cape Island on the Jersey coast to discover for themselves the delights of sea bathing.

In the early days before the big hotels, the city visitors came by boat, coach, and carriage—usually a two-day trip. Country people came too—wagonloads of fun seekers. They dipped and frolicked in the cold, foaming surf, dressed in a wild assortment of old clothes and hats—who needed a bathing suit? The visitors were boarded by the locals. Food was plentiful: a sheep to roast from a nearby farmer—corn from the fields—freshly caught fish and crabs from the sea. Old-fashioned country dancing and a lively fiddle made a happy scene.

Rowdy behavior was off limits at Cape May. Hotel boarders, paying up to ten dollars a week in the 1830s, were sometimes kept awake by "wild young men" drinking and carousing. Lacking recourse to town police, the natives formed a local vigilante group rousting the guilty ones from their rooms, usually at midnight. With a ringing of bells and clacking of carts the guilty were taken to the Society of Forker's quarters and "shaved" with a huge wooden razor.

In the 1840s and 1850s, Delaware steamboats began stopping daily instead of weekly. The liveliest spot at the Cape was the landing when the boats came in. Everybody dashed from the boat to waiting coaches, elbowing and crowding into seats—the men crushing the ladies' full skirts and suffering indignant eyes. Finally, luggage piled on, the coaches raced to town. The game was to get to the hotel counters first—the better the room, the bigger the tip for the driver.

With thousands of visitors coming in from eastern cities and from the south and west, rooms became critically short. Summer visitors were told, "Bring your own mattresses." Tents, sheds, parlors, and

Columbia Hotel, circa 1872.

A summer portrait, circa 1890. A child like this might have stayed at the Columbia Hotel, built in 1846 to accommodate six hundred—the aristocrat of Cape May. It prided itself on formality and ceremony; dinner was served at the fashionable hour of three instead of the usual one-thirty. On a summer afternoon music from the hotel band floated over the water while bathers splashed and played in the surf. The Columbia was destroyed in the fire of 1878.

Croquet on the lawn, Congress Hall, circa 1872. The Philadelphia photographer O. H. Willard combined business with pleasure when he set up his tent at Congress Hall. The sedate hotel life in Cape May contrasted sharply with the activity in nearby Atlantic City. The hotel's normal calm was shattered briefly in July of 1869 when the Philadelphia Grey Reserves serenaded President Grant on the hotel lawn. Congress Hall was the first hotel built in Cape May, in 1816, and was destroyed by the great fire of 1878.

kitchens were put to use after the hotel rooms were full. The scarcity of accommodations set off a hotel boom, and by 1856 Cape May had twenty-four hotels.

Henry Clay, the political darling of his time, visited the Mansion House almost every summer. When Clay arrived, word spread like wildfire and crowds of people came to see the great man. One year he was waylaid on the beach by ladies with scissors who snipped away at his hair, taking locks of it for keepsakes. (Locks of hair were in great demand—it mattered not whether a famous subject was alive or dead.) Both the Mansion House and the Mount Vernon were lost in the fire of 1857.

Hotels and boardinghouses took care to amuse their guests by having games nearby. Billiards and tenpins were old standbys, especially for rainy days. After supper everyone went out to promenade along the hard sand beach in the freshening breeze, the gentlemen with their after-dinner cigars, the ladies sparkling with their jewels. It was said of Cape May that "as day gives place to night, and the silver sheen of the moon dances on the water, there is as much spooning as ever a watering place can develop." The evening often ended with a "hop" paid for by a magnanimous hotel boarder who would hire a band and send out for refreshments.

Cape May had a pleasing combination of sea, pretty meadows, and salt-water creeks, with delightful spots for picnic parties. It was easy to find a driver and carriage—local farmers offered these services for a dollar. Favorite drives were to the lighthouse or to Higbee's Beach, where "Cape May diamonds" of pure crystal quartz washed by the sea could be found. A must for summer visitors was the five-mile drive to Cold Spring—a natural oddity, a clear, cool, spring in the midst of a

Two women in garden dresses and the two young sailors with their toy boats, opposite, might have stayed at the Stockton. The photographs passed into the hands of descendants in nearby Wilmington, Delaware.

The Stockton House, circa 1882. When the West Jersey Railroad came to Cape May after the Civil War, it bought a large track of oceanfront land. The Stockton House was built by the railroad at a cost of $600,000, with 475 rooms, an amusement center, and stables. The opening of the great hotel in 1869 was celebrated by an Inauguration Ball.

Centennial Pier, circa 1876. Cape May had several ocean piers frequented by fishermen and promenaders who liked to watch the rollers come in and to enjoy the wonderful smell of the sea. The boardwalk hugged close to the sand and was referred to as Flirtation Walk.

salt marsh. An octagonal building stood over the spring where a barman served drinks stronger than springwater, though some more pious visitors preferred the beverage prepared by God himself.

After the wearying Civil War years the resort had still another spurt of growth when the railroad came to town. Summertime pleasures were now but a few hours away by rail. With an eye to bringing in masses of pleasure seekers, the West Jersey Railroad bought a large tract of beach property in 1867. They put up a great excursion hotel for the overnighter and a luxury hotel called the Sea-Breeze with 100 baths, an oversized barroom, and a thousand feet of boardwalk leading to the beach. Cottages, too, multiplied—neat summer dwellings set in orderly rows on shady, narrow streets.

In the 1870s yachting became an important part of the vacation scene. Hundreds of sailing craft could be seen beyond the breakers, and at the inlets yachts lay in wait to take visitors sailing on the sound. The city became known for its regattas, bringing boats from Philadelphia, Baltimore, and New York. Steamboat companies now competed with the railroad for the Philadelphia trade. A new excursion house was built at the landing in 1878, and that year the new steamer, the *Republic,* made a nonstop trip from Philadelphia to Cape May in a little less than six hours. This was a good year for the Cape until November 9, when a great fire destroyed most of the big hotels, boardinghouses, and stores, as well as many homes. Cape May lay in ruins, an era vanished overnight.

On the beach at Cape May, circa 1870. Cape May boasted the widest beach on the Eastern seaboard with the softest, whitest sand.

Beach belle wringing out, circa 1895.

New hotels replaced the old, and within a year or two the town was almost back to normal. A visitor wrote about the resort in 1881: "Now the time is chiefly passed in bathing, and lounging about the hotels, and going to the station to see the train come in. Once in awhile the monotony is varied by the arrival of a bogus Lord from abroad who forgets to pay his bills, or by catching a shark and tying him to one of those little piers that the old ocean almost knocked to pieces last winter; but usually the effect of a prolonged visit to the Cape is the development of a ravenous appetite."

Hot and cold seawater baths had come to Cape May by the 1880s. In fact, it had the chief establishment of its kind in the country, Mr. William King's Excelsior Baths. The owner put in some extrawide bathtubs in 1881 for his "best developed" patrons. Now one could enjoy the ocean's tonic effect without the inconvenience of dipping in the ocean.

By the 1890s visiting summer resorts had become a popular excursion for bicycle clubs. Cyclists came in such numbers that Cape May passed an ordinance in 1896 to keep the speedsters down to eight miles an hour. With the bicycle craze came a local controversy. Some of the town ladies frowned on the "bloomer" styles and divided skirts worn by the girl cyclists and they formed an antibicycle club. One indignant young girl defended the costumes, saying, "Corsets fill more graves than whiskey!"

Cape May kept its prestige as a great summer resort despite the growing number of watering places along the New Jersey coast.

Atlantic City

"This portion . . . is covered with a beautiful growth of timber which is now being trimmed and the undergrowth removed, the lands graded and drained, and laid out in streets and walks which when completed, will render it very attractive. . . . The surface and beach are unsurpassed upon our coast. The ocean rolling in and breaking upon the beach for a distance of ten miles, the strand is entirely level and smooth and forms a drive of two hundred feet in width, so gentle is the slope."

These plans were unveiled by the speaker for the Camden & Atlantic Railroad's land company on July 1, 1854. The promoters had brought 600 of the most influential citizens of Philadelphia, Camden, and New York to spend a fun-filled day picnicking and touring the beach and adjoining lands.

Two years earlier, when railroad officials first visited Absecon Island, there had been only a few fishermen. Now some 1,000 acres of prime beach land, bought by the railroad's land company for $10 an acre, would soon sell for $100 to $300 an acre. And a contract had been let for the first wing of the United States Hotel, destined to be America's finest resort hotel in the 1850s.

After the boisterous building boom of the 1850s, the Civil War years and beyond brought a temporary quiet. The editor of *The Lady's Friend* wrote in 1868: "Atlantic City has the advantage for plain quiet folks that so many of its houses are kept by Friends. It is another Quaker City."

Whatever peace and quiet the Quakers brought came to an abrupt end when, on May 9, 1870, the city council voted funds to build its first boardwalk. The $5,000 needed for the walk was more than half the city's annual income. To get things started, the mayor made a cash loan of $1,080. Metropolitan newspapers hailed the boardwalk's opening as a great attraction, a road to sea breezes and health, a promenade on which to "see and be seen."

The Fortescue pavilion, 1882. The Fortescue Hotel provided its guests with a shaded retreat overlooking the ocean.

A boardwalk portrait, circa 1885.

Lifeguard, circa 1888. "Only the foolhearty need be saved in Atlantic City; so safe is the gently sloping beach." Nevertheless, competent lifeguards, surfboats, and equipment were very reassuring. The lifeguard boats usually rode on the ocean swells just beyond the bravest bathers.

Beach scene, 1896. To the heat-weary Philadelphian, summertime comfort in Atlantic City was only two hours away by fast train. On a hot Saturday, in as early as 1881, the three railroads might easily have carried thirteen thousand people to the pleasures of the resort.

The Epicycloidal Swing, circa 1879. One of the early wonders of Atlantic City, the swing was soon eclipsed by greater rides, beginning with the Ferris Wheel of 1892. Throughout the late 1800s, shell shops, tintype photographers, oyster stands, cheap dining lean-tos, and innumerable booths and rides multiplied along the new and ever wider boardwalk of Atlantic City. However, the devout were not forgotten. Until 1897 they gathered, some three thousand strong, in the merry-go-round casino and, seated on rocking chairs and benches, sang old-fashioned hymns.

A hot Saturday in Philadelphia could overtax the railroads so badly that boxcars with benches would be pressed into service. The flood of humanity would engulf the "excursion houses" and overflow into the saloons, restaurants, bathhouses, and amusement places.

The excursion houses were just the thing for a big spender with a small pocketbook. Clustered in rows near the inlet, they put up the overnighter and specialized in delicious dinners of freshly caught seafood. Many of the houses were owned by the railroads and rented for eight thousand dollars a season, still attracting families despite the high price.

The area around the excursion houses was not one of peace and quiet. All day long the merry-go-rounds hummed and their steam organs pierced the air with strident renderings of "Lilly and the Rose"

43

The Traymore Hotel, 1883. The Traymore could accommodate up to five hundred guests willing to pay from $3 to $5 a day for beachfront pleasures and an endless round of social events.

and the "Washington Post March," punctuated by yells and screams from the riders of swings as high as a house.

Atlantic City had its aristocratic area, on the southerly side of town. Big hotels sat close to the beachfront, and on the back streets stood rows of villas and cottages all set on neat brick pilings. Hotels had early become the social life of the city with their nightly dances and "hops." Hired bands played afternoon and evening concerts; imported entertainers gave evening shows and skits.

Each year brought more and more hotels, both plain and fancy, worth ten million dollars by the century's end. The four-star hotels of the 1890s, open all year, like the Windsor and Randolph, were known even to the dandies of Europe. The Randolph offered the comforts of home or better, with steam heat, open fireplaces, elevator service, rooms with private bath and toilet, and even its own electricity plant.

Meanwhile, the city council's boardwalk gamble paid off handsomely. Stories captioned "The Boardwalk, Atlantic City" were flooding big-city newspapers. Other seaside resorts were quick to copy the idea with boardwalks of their own. On April 16, 1876, the city fathers held their first Easter Parade on the boardwalk. The sun smiled on Atlantic City that day, and so did the vast numbers of people who came to watch the Gilded Age promenade of eye-filling parasoled darlings displaying their form-fitting finery of ruffles and lace.

The original boardwalk was in a sad state of disrepair by 1880 and was rebuilt. This new boardwalk was swept into the sea by a giant winter storm four years later, then rebuilt and again destroyed by a

*"Float me, Charlie," circa 1899.
Bathhouses for rent dotted the west side of
the boardwalk and an up-to-date bathing
suit could be rented by the hour or the day.
A tunnel under the boardwalk brought the
bather to the beach and the ocean, where
the water temperature in August ranged
from 70° to an ideal 80°.*

Bathing in the surf, circa 1883.

hurricane in 1889, taking with it the bathhouses, restaurants, and stores along it as well.

The fourth boardwalk opened in the spring of 1890. The walk was now twenty-four feet wide and stood ten feet above the sand, with handrails, esplanades with a view of the ocean to the east, and buildings on the west. Gone was the annual Atlantic City news flash: "Nearly every day somebody falls off the boardwalk. In nearly every instance, the parties have been flirting." The boardwalk was big business during the nineties. New amusements moved in: the "giant ferris wheel," the "revolving observation tower" (125 feet high and ten cents to enter), and the "haunted swings" where squeals from the gentle sex were a sure-fire attraction. A new three-decker carousel was a world wonder, with a first-floor animal kingdom merry-go-round, second-floor skating rink, and third-floor theatre big enough to hold an orchestra and fifteen hundred dancers.

A view of docks, 1891. "Select a yacht from the numerous fleet that here spread their white canvas above trim models, and indulge in a sail. There is smooth inside sailing for the timid and rough outside for the daring," wrote Dr. Thomas K. Reed for Godey's Lady Book *in 1875.*

One hour's catch, 1891. Weakfish, striped bass, porgies, mackerel, bluefish—according to local publicity, all were just waiting for the sport fisherman. Each morning at ten-thirty, the big net on the fishing pier was brought ashore and often, to the delight of the onlookers, was filled with fish and oddities of the sea—puffballs, spider crabs, stingarees, and small sharks.

The boardwalk was Atlantic City and Atlantic City was the boardwalk, so said the council when they made it an official street in 1896. This was the year they built still another new boardwalk, forty feet wide with underpinnings of steel.

The changes wrought in the nineties did not alter the character of the boardwalk; it was still a stroller's paradise. The promenader could still enjoy the bracing ocean air and smell the inviting aromas of cooking candies, apples on a stick, saltwater taffy, hot dogs loaded with mustard relishes, and the tangy odor of sarsaparilla and root beer. Potpourri shops were still there for vacation keepsakes of pillows, gifts, and bric-a-brac stamped "Atlantic City."

Ocean Grove

Under the umbrella, circa 1891. Out-of-town church groups came by the thousands to Ocean Grove for camp meetings. The lady on the left looks as though she is ready for more worldly pleasures.

cean Grove—the mile-long oceanfront bordered by two pretty lakes—was founded by a small group of Methodist clergymen and their friends who first pitched their tents in the wilderness in 1869. Before the first summer was out there was a din of hammers and saws as the wild woods began to be tamed. Streets were laid out with names taken from well-known Methodists or from the Bible. Cottages began dotting the landscape and over 100 tents, rented from the Ocean Grove Camp Meeting Association, were arranged in friendly groupings in true camp-meeting style. Rowboats appeared on Wesley Lake, and for those who enjoyed sea bathing a few bathhouses were constructed. Of course all bathers had to be suitably covered. A total of 373 of the little lots, 30 by 60 feet, were sold with 99-year leases by year's end to "people of good moral character." By 1880 lot values had soared 1,000 percent.

How to avoid the usual sins of a watering place? The association had the answer—outlaw intoxicating liquors, but don't stop at that—lock up the town entrance gates on Saturday night, except for footpaths, and allow no bathing, boating, or driving on Sunday. The Ocean Grove Camp Meeting Association had the power to make its own laws, and it exercised its full power. Anyone interfering with the peace and religious tone of the town was run off in a hurry or arrested; pack peddlers, eyeglass peddlers, organ grinders were quickly ushered out of town. Soon the association cracked down not only on peddlers and tramps but also on Punch-and-Judy shows, bird shows, gymnastics, brass bands, and religious frauds. Dogs were required to be muzzled—unmuzzled dogs were held for twenty-four hours and shot. In fact, it was wise to leave dogs at home.

Even the founders of the association were surprised that their town with its strict regulations should flourish in such liberal times. Within ten years, twenty thousand people at a time were often in the small town during the summer season.

The heart of the town was the auditorium where the August camp

Tent life in Ocean Grove, 1873. Hundreds of tents like this one dotted the grounds near the auditorium, the center of religious activity in Ocean Grove. The auditorium was open on all sides with a preacher's platform and an area outside kept clear for benches and chairs when the crowds overflowed. In 1894 a new auditorium, seating ten thousand people, was built.

"Surf-meeting," circa 1883. Thousands of people gathered to worship at the water's edge on Sabbath mornings. For the afternoons there were the bathing beaches at each end of Ocean Grove. Bathhouses were available for 75 cents a day or $4.50 a week, and bathing suits were rented by the hour, a card stamped with the time pinned to the suit.

meeting and daily religious services were held. Here thousands came to hear famous preachers orating in traditional God-fearing camp-meeting style, and the warm summer air rang with soul-stirring music. Popular concert artists and singers came to thrill the huge crowds. To house the great streams of visitors at the height of the season, little tent cottages were rented out by the association. These provided spartan living in an era of Victorian finery, but to the summer visitor it must have been a welcome relief to turn to light housekeeping. The furnished rooms, eleven by eighteen or thirteen by eighteen feet, had a tent on the front, with a floor, and rented for $2.50 a week or $75.00 and up for the season.

Without the railroads Ocean Grove might not have been the success it was. A New Yorker could board a train from the city at 5:00 A.M. and two hours later arrive in Ocean Grove in time for breakfast. The round-trip excursion ticket cost only $1.85, breakfast at the hotel was 50 cents, and if the visitor stayed on for dinner it was an additional 75 cents. An excursionist of modest means could go rowing on Wesley Lake or go to the beach, south to the Lillagore bathhouses and pavilion or north to Ross's, both of which had bathing suits for rent. And although visitors to Ocean Grove could not find a barroom, they could easily find an ice-cream parlor—there were five in town.

Boating on the lakes in the little boats ornamented with brightly colored cushions, striped awnings, and flags was one of the romantic pleasures of Ocean Grove. At night the boats were a pretty sight with gay paper lanterns hung in strings and clusters.

In the summer of 1888, new revenues for the Association came from two toll bridges replacing the old ferryboat. It cost a passenger a penny to cross over from Asbury Park. Tolls from the two bridges brought in a profit of about two thousand dollars over a twelve-week period.

The Ocean Grove people were almost as fervently patriotic as they were religious. In 1876, the year of the great centennial, a grand celebration was held on the Fourth, complete with large parades in Ocean Grove and Asbury Park. In the march to the auditorium were two military companies, members of the Ocean Grove Association, and Asbury Park officials. A free lunch was one of the highlights of the day.

In sharp contrast to the strict and often fanatical outlook of the people in Ocean Grove was the uninhibited behavior of the local Jersey

The Lakeview House, circa 1878. Everyone turned out to pose with the big brass band. A new visitor to Ocean Grove was soon informed that respectable people retired from the beach at ten-thirty in the evening. Lights went out at midnight.

folk. Inland farmers, and townspeople, they came to the beach once a year, by wagon and train, for a day of sea bathing and fun. Just when Big Sea Day, also called Salt Water Day, came about, none of the old-timers knew, but all said it was a very old custom. Some said a circus element had crept in; the city people came to laugh and the townsfolk came for profit. An eyewitness in 1892 wrote of the day:

"Parked upon the soft yellow sand were hundreds and hundreds of carriages. Beyond them were groups of tents and booths, and beyond them the sea. Swarming around these teams and booths, drinking red lemonade, eating peanuts, courting and visiting, were the blond freckled Jerseymen and Jerseywomen. In unabashed freedom walked the bathers, in dresses of every sort and length and color; and they were not all young. Old men [were] in suits of field clothes. Lovers walked along hand in hand. Ordinary rules of conduct seemed not to hold. All

Wesley Lake, circa 1874. Boating was a pleasure all ages could enjoy. According to a local newspaper, boats could be purchased for $15 to $100.

was decorous, but all was hilarious. They forgot care, false modesty, age, youth, social distinctions.''

The observer reported that as the day wore on the crowd became more animated. Hundreds bathed, dozens of men pulled off their shoes and plunged into the cold surf, horseplay went on in the breakers, and a bottle was passed about. Dancers continued to swing their partners in unabated frenzy, lemonade flowed, and nickel games of chance found more takers. About the roaring crowd the air was clear, hot, and sweet, and the blue green ocean shore with blue-hulled ships was silhouetted against the horizon. The crowd gradually began to thin, for it was a long journey home.

By 1900 Ocean Grove was packed tightly with houses on small lots, there were more than 200 hotels, and its camp-meeting site had become the largest of its kind in the world.

Asbury Park

Much of New Jersey's wild seacoast lay undeveloped in the summer of 1870. It was quite by chance that James A. Bradley, in the late spring of that year, came down from New York City for a rest amid the pines and sand, pitching his tent in the quiet wilderness of Ocean Grove. From the vantage point of his tent he speculated on the land across the lake and mused—was it for him? He found that the parcel of land just north of Ocean Grove—some 500 acres of briars and scrub pines fronting on the ocean—could be had for a mere $90,000. He had a feeling that he could mold the land into a superb summer resort for upper-class Christian citizens who wished a quiet watering place without the tomblike silence of Ocean Grove. To round things off, a railroad now linked the land with metropolitan New York.

Bradley purchased his land in the fall of 1870 and began planning an elite resort where the less pious could summer without the strait-laced code that Ocean Grove imposed. He named it Asbury Park in honor of Francis Asbury, the father of Methodism in America. In tune with the temperance movement of the time Bradley hated liquor, and he made its prohibition a deed restriction. His friends thought he went too far: "With your restriction [whiskey] you can never make a seaside resort a success so near to New York." Not a whit abashed, Bradley called his critics "the timid and the croakers."

Founder Bradley (a title he dearly loved) was a man with imagination. Being a latecomer to the scene, he could survey the mistakes and discomforts of other Jersey resort towns. He proudly laid out Asbury Park's new streets and brought in shade trees to line the broad avenues. He left open spaces for parks, walks, and a mile-long ocean promenade. Fifteen miles of pipes brought pure water to each household. Every lot had a sanitary sewer connection. Neat clusters of bathing houses were spaced along the beach—bathing attire was prohibited on city streets.

Eldridge Park, Elmira, N.Y., circa 1874.

Ice-cream stand, Sunset Lake, 1876. This little island retreat was located in the quiet north end of Asbury Park. The casino and pier were the pleasure centers of the resort and on weekends and holidays were packed by the thousands.

A view of Asbury Park, circa 1881. The growth of Asbury Park was fantastic. From the scrub pine and brier barren of 1871, it became an attractive resort with about fifteen thousand summer residents by 1881 and a favorite vacation spot for the best families of New York, Philadelphia, and Washington by the end of the century. Accommodating up to twenty-five thousand visitors at one time, Asbury Park was known as a good place to hold conventions and outings.

In 1877 Bradley brought to town the prestigious Education Hall which had been a showplace in the Philadelphia Centennial of 1876. A large opera house seating some fifteen hundred people was built to further cultural pursuits, an opportunity which obviously must have fallen on deaf ears, since in 1887 theatrical producers McGeachy and Comstock left town in disgust after losing several thousand dollars.

Under the benign and watchful eye of its founder the city emerged as an important resort. An 1881 visitor said, "It is a town much like Atlantic City in appearance; but more soil and trees and less bare sand . . . Here are thousands of modest cottages and a large number of new ones building . . . and in the height of its season has at least fifteen thousand inhabitants." Asbury Park was often called a small replica of Atlantic City, but the two cities differed sharply. Asbury Park did not have the carnival air of Atlantic City; no puffing locomotives chugged up its streets on the way to excursion houses. For the fun and thrill seekers Asbury Park was certainly dull—no saloons, no big wheels, only the merry-go-round and the toboggan chute.

When it came to publicity, Asbury Park could beat the drum just as loudly as Atlantic City. Asbury Park's important doings now appeared in big-city newspapers, although its news was undoubtedly less sensational. The big news from Asbury Park was motherhood. Nowhere was the term mother held in more reverence. In the 1890s the town fathers came up with a gala affair that could not lose—an annual boardwalk baby parade with prizes and souvenirs for all entrants.

A Pennsylvania Railroad booklet summed up the town's character in 1898: "Asbury Park holds a distinct place among the many resorts. . . . It is pre-eminently the resort of that better class whose tastes are cultivated and whose methods of enjoyment bear the stamp of their own high characters."

56

A boardwalk portrait, circa 1885.

Long Branch

The United States Hotel, Long Branch, circa 1881. This three-hundred-room hotel, located midway along Ocean Drive, was on the quiet side. And, as the story of 1881 ran, it was the hotel where two pug dogs belonging to a female guest were brought to the "nurse's hall" three times a day and fed the best of everything on a silver platter.

Mansion House, 1873. Laird's mammoth boardinghouse was opened in 1846, long before the term American Plan came into vogue. President Grant often took part in the gala social events there.

Long Branch history as a summering place dates back to 1788 when Philadelphia visitors came in sailing sloops and were brought to shore by local fishing boats. By 1838 visitors were already reporting the "once-delightful resort going downhill." Philadelphia people still came. Rules were still strict—no cardplaying or billiards—but two ninepin alleys were opened and women were allowed. The big event during the 1838 season was a pig-catching tournament with the prize—the pig and a purse of gold. The contest was held in an enclosed field and crowds of spectators and vehicles of all kinds were at the scene. At the shout "Let go the pig!" a large greased animal trotted about the field. The "knights," local Jersey lads and fishermen, tried to "head in" the pig. The only trouble was that the winner was a black, one of the hotel help, and none of the other contestants were pleased to be outdone. A big row ensued, women fainted, and not until darkness fell did the free-for-all calm down.

By 1847 New York society was coming to the resort, easy to reach by steamboat, the last four miles being made by coach or wagon. Philadelphians had a more difficult journey, crossing the state by stagecoach, a long, monotonous, sandy ride. Long Branch had one large hotel, on a sandy bluff high above the beach. On the edge of the bluff were little arbors, shaded with greens and furnished with seats, peaceful places where the vista of ocean and beach could be seen for miles.

By 1876 the town looked "not unlike a circus." One visitor described Ocean Drive in late afternoon:

"Fast flying horses, driven by men in livery . . . numberless flags in brightest red, white, and blue flutter from liberty poles on lawns and hotel tops . . . brass-bands blare on the grassy lawns, and here and there side-show-like tents for the sale of pop and gingerbread or practice with air-guns at striped targets flap their canvas sides in the breeze . . ."

58

The Race at Monmouth Park, 1872. Monmouth Park, where the Jersey Derby was held, was a short twenty-five-cent ride backcountry from Long Branch. The system of betting by mutuel pools, introduced here in the 1870s, was "openly indulged in by many ladies as well as gentlemen who have been taught to look upon gambling as a terrible vice . . . and would be horrified at the thought of joining the throng in Chamberlin's club-house . . . but who go without a qualm to the races at Monmouth Park and bet their money on the running of horses instead of on the turn of a card."

Hoey's house and garden, circa 1875. "The crowning glory of Long Branch ... is the estate of John Hoey where about one hundred acres are laid out as a garden and park. Statuary greets the eye in all directions.... The roads wind around among the flower beds and through the groves and lawns.... To maintain this great floral establishment requires a large force of gardeners and the hot houses consume coal by the train-load." Like the barons of old, Mr. Hoey could survey his estate from his mansion. To alert the small army of employees, a flag flew over the house when the master was in residence.

All sorts were seen at the resort—money moguls, political bigwigs, artists and actors (a theatrical colony summered here), and the less-well-to-do. Long Branch had a republican spirit about it not often seen. Hot summer Sundays brought huge crowds of excursionists by train from the city—many of the lower class, including a sprinkling of rough characters and sharpies.

President Grant had earlier been persuaded by shrewd capitalists to accept a handsome summer cottage in Long Branch. Once it was know that the resort would be the summer home of the President, "villa plots sold like the proverbial hot cakes." Farms were bought for thirty or forty dollars an acre and promoters turned cornfields into lots. Existing hotels put on new additions. New York reporters were enticed down to the resort to write about the city's gaiety and charm even when things were dull. Champagne was in the air. Lots selling one summer for $500 skyrocketed to $5,000 the following season. Cheap hotels and boardinghouses catered to modest pocketbooks, and well-dressed dandies seen at hotel "hops" sometimes disappeared, like Cinderella, to more modest quarters at midnight. A plush gambling establishment, Chamberlin's Clubhouse, was near the elegant West End Hotel and within sight of the President's cottage. Here in smoke-filled rooms Wall Street tycoons played at the roulette and gaming tables.

Bathing was for everybody. When the hotel or cottage people saw a white flag flying they knew beach conditions were good. A note of warning was given: ladies were cautioned not to be near the bluff or beach before 6:00 A.M. because men were allowed to bathe then in less-than-regulation costume.

President Grant's Cottage, Elberon, 1873. The dark red roof of the "summer capital of the United States" during Grant's term of office overlooked the ocean, south of Long Branch, on Ocean Drive. Of a summer's evening, one could see "doors and windows all wide open, and the interior furnishing glimpses of a comfortable but not showy home, with pictures and books about and lamps burning."

Grand Ball in honor of President Grant at the Stetson House, 1869. Congress often complained that Grant spent too much time away from Washington. Grant loved to make a summer's evening round in the Long Branch hotels—a banquet at one, a soirée at another, and a ball at a third. He was always welcomed as the hero of the evening.

It was in August 1879 that Captain Boyton began his much-publicized swim to Coney Island and the beach crowd at both resorts eagerly awaited the outcome. He struck out at 3:30 P.M. on a Saturday and finally arrived at Coney Island on Sunday at 8:00 P.M., after battling rough water, fatigue, and sharks.

Just as bathing was a popular morning pastime, drives were the high fashion in the afternoon. One of the most popular jaunts was to a little settlement called Pleasure Bay, on a branch of the Shrewsbury River. The most important people came to Pleasure Bay. It was a rich man's playground, with sailing regattas and famous clambakes sometimes attended by the President. Standing in a grove of trees was an old-fashioned tavern called Old Pleasure Bay House, which had private supper rooms to hire for mixed parties and a bar supplied with choice wines, liquors, and cigars.

Outside, the less sophisticated sat at weather-beaten picnic tables and watched sailing yachts bringing people to the opposite shore, where a favorite pastime was catching crabs with a net and a piece of fish on the end of a stick. After sailing there was often a clambake, a local delight with "green corn, clams, crabs, potatoes, yellow-legged

Leland's Ocean Hotel, 1873. Long Branch had some of the largest resort hotels in the world. The West End Hotel, on the south end of Ocean Drive, could put up some fifteen hundred people. Not far behind was the older Ocean Hotel with a capacity of eight hundred. But when it came to social snobbery, Leland's stood at the top of the list, with name bands, concerts, and glittering fancy dances.

Pleasure Railroad, Ocean Hotel, 1873. This pleasure railroad was the granddaddy of the miniature steam locomotives and cars so popular at later amusement centers.

Bathing scene, circa 1865.

chickens, and sometimes pigeons,'' and then a drive home in the moonlight.

In the evening, dancing parties were held in the spacious parlors of the big hotels, often varied by concerts and amateur theatricals. Saturday night dances were the pinnacle of social events during the season, the hotel piazzas jammed with elegantly clad guests who sat by open windows listening to the music and watching the dancers. At midnight, sometimes a group of partygoers went on to serenade the President or some other notable.

By the 1880s the beaches north and south of town had filled in with other fashionable resorts. At the settlement of Monmouth Beach the seaside cottages had handsome stables, ''the horses, in many cases, having as fine houses as their owners.''

Social life was very active among the summer villa owners. Many people had their own tennis courts and gave lawn parties and dances, the grounds alight with Chinese lanterns and elaborate floral decorations.

Long Branch and its neighbors, with money pouring in from New York for palatial hotels and villas, had become resorts for the wealthier class. But fashion and vice walked hand in hand. One visitor in 1889 wrote, ''not a place for [the] circumspect parent to take [the] family.''

Feeding the swans in Central Park.

New Yorkers' Playgrounds

One of the delightful summer rambles for New Yorkers in mid-nineteenth century was to promenade the walks of Castle Garden, where once the ancient fortress stood on the margin of the Battery grounds. After losing its military character in 1823, Castle Garden became a popular amusement place where on summer nights the air resounded with music of concert and opera—and it was here that Jenny Lind, the famed Swedish opera star, charmed her audiences in 1850. The Battery continued throughout the century to attract strollers who enjoyed the ocean vistas and sea breezes. Water craft of all descriptions, bearing flags of all nations, could be seen; many an hour could be whiled away by those who loved the sea.

Even earlier, residents enjoyed all of the cooling delights of saltwater bathing at the New-York Floating Baths, a bathing establishment moored at Castle Garden. The *Knickerbocker* magazine in May of 1839 announced that the "floating baths" contributed to the health of perhaps a million sea bathers who could swim in "spacious reservoirs of pure salt sea-brine." An 1840 advertisement in the same publication read: "Let every man, who would know the luxury of Health; firmly-braced nerves, hearty appetite, and a clear head; visit our friend Dr. Rabineau's Salt Water Floating Baths."

Nathaniel P. Willis wrote in 1844 about summer pleasures: "Smile those who have private yachts! We know no pleasanter trip after the dusk of the evening, than to stroll down to the ferry, haul a bench to the bow of the ferry-boat, and 'open up' the evening breeze for two miles and back, for a shilling . . . Try this, of a hot evening, all who prefer coolness and have a mind that is good company."

Many city dwellers agreed and disembarked on Staten Island at St. George where railroad transit provided transportation about the island. The drives about the hills were attractive, and from the heights were magnificent overlooks of harbor and ocean. New Brighton was the largest village, and it

Meadowbrook Hunt Club, Long Island, 1892. In their pursuit of English activities and English manners, the New York elite soon discovered fox hunting. Although George Washington and his fellow Virginians had been early American devotees of the sport, it was not until 1875 that members of the New York Social Register began importing dogs from England for the chase. Over the next twenty years, hunt clubs were established within easy distance from the city—Westchester, Long Island, and New Jersey. Meadowbrook, near Hempstead, had a pack of twenty-six dogs for the chase by 1892.

Floating Baths, A View in the Bay of New York, circa 1858. Dr. Rabineau's saltwater baths, just off the tip of lower Manhattan, fell out of fashion by the late 1850s as Coney Island and other new places attracted holiday crowds.

contained fine summer hotels and handsome villas. Staten Island was also the home of the fashionable Livingston Cricket Club, haunt of the sporting set.

Willis also apprised his readers of the delights of an "airing after dinner," the dinner hour in that era being about 3 P.M.: "We step out from our side-street to the brink of Broadway, and presto, like magic, up drives an empty coach with two horses, red-velvet lining, and windows open ... The main difference between us and the rich man, for that hour, is, that he rides in a green lane, and we on Broadway—he sees green leaves and we pretty women—he pays much and we pay little ..."

In 1858 a beautiful new playground for New Yorkers began to arise from ash rock, "a desert of rubbish with neither lawns or foliage, the abiding place of colonies of shantie-squatters." It was to become Central Park. With enormous energy, a great deal of money and an army of three to four thousand men, a lovely park of 843 acres was created with green stretches of

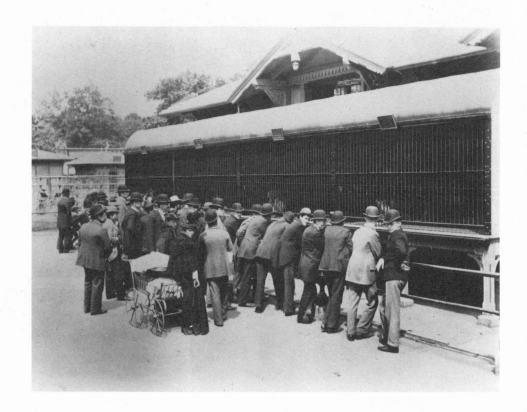

The Menagerie at Central Park on a summer afternoon, circa 1895.

Two ladies at Central Park Lake, circa 1895. A gondola ride was one of the pleasures of New York on a summer's day.

West Drive, Central Park, 1895. Carriages and promenaders passed the statue of Daniel Webster near the boat pond and the Sheep Meadow.

Central Park, The Drive, 1862. "The almost total exclusion of the outer world, and the production of effects of distance, are really remarkable triumphs of landscape gardening," wrote a visitor to Central Park not long after its opening.

meadow, trees, flowers, lakes, and winding drives that would bring new life and pleasure to the city.

Gradually as the work progressed on the park, under the supervision of landscape architects Frederick Law Olmsted and Calvert Vaux, roads were laid, rocks drilled, drains dug, trees planted, bridges built. Work continued throughout the century and finally the park offered enjoyment for every taste—for the quiet stroller, there were asphalt walks winding among trees, over hills, to the lakes and shady arbors; bridle paths for horseback riding; playgrounds and merry-go-rounds for children; ball fields, tennis courts, museums, art galleries, and even an animal menagerie.

In the morning and evening hours the park was alive with visitors. Young riders came out for their constitutional jog at daybreak and older riders quietly pounded along the paths, oblivious of the stares of pedestrians. But most of all the pedestrians enjoyed watching the graceful carriages and the pretty wagons that passed by—"some of the light trotting wagons so gaily painted that they flash along like sunbeams on cobwebs." When the bicycle craze came in during the 1880s and 1890s, the bicyclists, too, joined the busy throng. And for those who stopped to rest were seats enough for ten thousand people, scattered along the driveways!

One of the attractions that delighted child and adult alike was the wooden swan boats on the pond, near the Fifty-ninth

Boys swimming off the East River Fulton Fish Market pier amongst bowsprits of cargo schooners, 1892.

Street entrance. The boats moved over the water without a ripple. "They pass bold rocks, sharp points of land, and wooded shores, and disappear under bridges and glide silently into shady bays so narrow that the foliage of the trees on the banks almost meets above the water."

Central park offered fresh air for those who could not go to the seaside, green leaves, birds, and many forms of nature for those who could not go to the mountains. Many in the 1890s regarded the park as the eighth wonder of the world!

Fashionable New York clubs were the haven of the very rich, and for summertime excursions nothing could compare to the activities of the New York Yacht Club, an institution dating from 1844. Here the famous names in yachting—the boating set and naval officers—all spun yarns about feats of the past. The squadron cruises of the club were popular—their stopping places Huntington, Long Island; New London, Connecticut; and Newport, Rhode Island, where races for the cups were the great attractions.

Thousands of more ordinary folk escaped the hot and dusty city by taking the commodious steamers of the 1860s, which brought passengers every hour of the summer through the whole length of the Harlem River, from Harlem under the High Bridge of the Croton Aqueduct to the vicinity of King's Bridge. The whole trip, by boats or railroad and boat, cost but ten or twelve cents each way.

69

Livingston Cricket Club, Staten Island, 1894. On Sundays, ferryboats left the city every forty-five minutes for St. George on Staten Island, where the Rapid Transit Railroad ran south to Cricket Club Station in Livingston. The Cricket Club was where the fashionable members of New York society could meet for a game of lawn tennis in the 1890s. Lawn tennis had been sport for the kings of England—no commoners allowed—for six hundred years before it was introduced in America in the late 1870s.

High Bridge, by which the Croton Aqueduct was carried across the Harlem River, was a favorite spot for excursionists out for a day's outing. The Harlem steamers landed in front of High Bridge, and the pleasure seekers poured out with their picnic baskets to seek the coolness of the surrounding woods and meadows, or they climbed the hill to cross the aqueduct to the opposite shore.

Among other favorite haunts for a summer's day was a ride out to McCombs Dam where two excellent hotels dispensed food and pleasure to their patrons. Soft-shell crabs and oysters were favorites, and boating and fishing were added inducements.

For the wealthy New Yorkers who did not wish to travel long distances, steamers could take them to watering places like Bath, about eight miles from New York, or farther out on Long Island to Oyster Bay, still a modest resort in late century, where bathing and fishing were excellent and accommodations the best. Also nearby New Jersey offered attractive resorts.

The most fashionable nearby resort of the 1850s was Rockaway Beach, eight miles south of Jamaica and twenty miles from New York, reached by railroad and stage. An impressive oceanfront hotel had been built in 1834 called Marine Pavilion. Among other "houses" in the vicinity was Rock Hall, built near the beach and a favorite with sea bathers.

By the 1880s, the resort picture again changed. Rockaway Beach became cheap and tawdry, while other places became quiet family resorts. Babylon was in the 1880s one of the most fashionable resorts for wealthy New Yorkers on the island. Those wanting the seclusion of Fire Island and a good hotel went by train to Bayside and from there took a steamer across South Bay.

Visitors going to the vicinity of Roslyn rode on the Glen Cove branch of the railroad. Two miles beyond Roslyn was a camp-meeting resort situated on a bluff overlooking the Sound, with a large hotel, cottages, and a camp-meeting tabernacle. Beyond Sea Cliff was Glen Cove with its highly popular Pavilion Hotel. (These resorts could also be reached by steamer.) The railroad terminated at Locust Valley, stages ran four miles to the old summer resort of Oyster Bay. Also, many farmhouses accommodated visitors at modest rates. Beyond Hicksville the main line ran due east to Farmingdale, Brentwood, Central Islip, and Lakeland. Stages continued to Yaphank and the pretty village of Center Moriches.

Coney Island

Marine Railway Station, Coney Island, circa 1880. The narrow gauge "Marine Railway" shuttled between Brighton Beach and Manhattan Beach. Its cost of construction was paid for in a single season by the nickel fare charged for the open-air ride.

Engerman's Piazza, circa 1878.

"It does not seem likely ever to be a restful place of peaceful, meditative order."—An 1880 visitor

"This favorite sea-bathing resort, ten miles south of the city of New York, is reached by steamers and stages. . . . The beach is much resorted to during the summer months for sea-air and bathing. . . . There are two or three well-kept public houses . . . where can be enjoyed the finest bathing imaginable. A drive on the beach is delightful; the sand is so fine and compact as to form a perfect carriage way. The shores and inlets abound with crabs, clams, oysters, and waterfowl." So stated J. Disturnell's guidebook in 1855.

In the days before the Civil War Coney Island was still asleep, and the list of notables who had visited there was indeed slim. New York's fashionable were installed and well watered in nearby Rockaway Beach at the Marine Pavilion Hotel with its forty-four prestigious Greek columns. Coney Island was still twenty years away from the ambush of a high-priced hotel. In the late 1850s a pavilion and bathing house went up on the west beach, and around the mid-sixties a few restaurants, food stands, and a sleepy railroad were established.

Then New Yorkers made a startling discovery: Coney Island, which had been there all the time, was right under their noses. City newspapers leaped on the bandwagon giving publicity, and overnight the lowly Coney Island clam rose to new heights among gastronomic delicacies. Chowder, steamers, and clams on the half-shell! City people struck out for the island by land and sea, by horsecar, railroad and boat. New restaurants, hotels, saloons, and bath pavilions began popping up by the score on the island. Fortunes could be made exploiting the Coney clam. Small hotel and restaurant men were rubbing shoulders with the best of New York's sharpies, and the noisy excursionist, out for a day of fun and chowder, was the target.

Group of young women in bathing dress, circa 1888. After the Civil War, the latest bathing dresses were "drawers, fastened at the ankle, and a tunic made with a yoke, night-gown fashion, reaching to the knee, and confined at the waist by a belt . . . the majority dress in gray . . . some in black, some in scarlet, many in sailor blue . . . broad-brimmed straw hats may be decorated with large chenille balls. . . ." A description from The Lady's Friend, *1868.*

Brighton Pier, Steamer Taurus, Coney Island, 1887. In the 1880s, excursion steamers brought millions of people to Coney Island for a dip in the ocean or a stroll on the beach. The trip from New York City took about forty-five minutes. By the end of the century, Coney Island's problem had become people—there were more per square foot of beach than any resort in the world.

"Ah there!" 1897.

Gypsy dancer, 1897.

Coney Island pleasure boat, circa 1890.

A contest began between the entrenched summer resorters and the day excursionists and through the seventies the resorter retreated to the still-barren east end of the island. Their outposts were the snobbish hotels, each more formidable than the last, with imposing towers and turrets. By 1880 the island had split into several colonies sharply divided by social caste. Norton's Point on the west end became a haunt of the low-brow where the toughs and ladies of the night bedded down.

Eastward was West Brighton Beach, a throbbing center of pleasure for the ordinary day excursionist. Here was the great iron pier with its massive bathing pavilions and eating houses busy enough to keep two thousand waiters on the move. Here was the home of the fat boy, nine feet around the waist, the Punch-and-Judy shows, the flying horses and giant swings, shooting galleries, flags, and big signs—all blending to music from seven big orchestras, small bands, organs, and the sounds of people at play. Two showpieces left over from the 1876 Philadelphia Centennial had been moved to West Brighton. The Machinery Hall was renamed the Sea Beach Palace and turned into a hotel and railroad station. The other prize was a three-hundred-foot-high observation tower that was for the moment Coney's pride and joy.

The clam was still served everywhere in its many guises but its days were numbered. The hot dog, born and bred in West Brighton, was on its way up.

The next step up the social ladder eastward was the colony at Brighton Beach, a playground for the pseudofashionable of Coney Island. This was the home of the Brighton Hotel, the first of the big wooden monsters featuring long shaded piazzas and a view of the sea. It touted the European Plan, an idea for "raising the price of board by installments . . . the only thing to be got on the elaborate bill of fare for less than a dollar was clam chowder." The hotel's rates were two dollars per day upward. The two-dollar room commanded a fine view of the graveled roofs of the hotel's kitchens and a half dozen railways leading across the marshes toward the distant hills of Brooklyn.

Manhattan Beach, the most fashionable of the colonies and the home away from home for much of New York society, was about a third of a mile east of Brighton Beach. It was here that New York's "better" people (not quite the upper crust) came to water by the week, month, or season. Two enormous hotels dominated this section of the island, the plush Manhattan Beach Hotel and the sedate Oriental Hotel, a refuge with privacy and soft music where French nursemaids wearing outlandish dresses cared for toddling infants. At the Oriental the tired "swell" from the city could enjoy bathing in the ocean under electric lights and then dress in the elaborate twenty-seven-hundred-square-foot bathhouse amid the conveniences of foot tubs and plate-glass mirrors. It was rumored about that two thousand wet bathing suits an hour could pass along the endless belt on their way to be washed in the bathhouse laundry. People in the know said that either of the big hotels

In the surf, 1891.

Man diving, 1899.

The Razzle Dazzle, 1896. Coney Island changed in the 1890s. "Aurally it is a riot of noises of roller coasters, from two to six stories high; of test-your-lung machines; of shooting galleries . . . of those strange merry-go-rounds . . . of razzle-dazzle rings that go all ways at once, like a ship's compass . . . of rocking-boat devises that would make Neptune seasick if he rode them . . . of hand organs, of yelling sea-bathers; in short, of pandemonium."

Manhattan Beach Hotel, circa 1877. "They have charming parlors and piazza promenades reserved to them, and jealously guarded from intrusion, in an upper story." The Manhattan Beach Hotel was set apart from the noise and excitement of West Brighton Beach. Built in 1877, the sprawling hotel had an oceanfront of one-eighth of a mile and was probably the only hotel in the country to have a jail in its basement.

had to take in at least $5,000 a day to break even. The Manhattan Beach Hotel had exclusive shops like the brightly colored booth of the fruit seller or the seashell jewelry shop with its glass cases.

As early as 1880 the heyday of Coney Island's long-staying visitor was nearly over. Already Coney Island was billed as the biggest amusement resort in the world with the biggest and best of thrill rides found anywhere. Its destiny lay in the nickel ride (by the nineties it became the ten-cent ride). The resort's future lay in providing a big-time outing for "regular" New Yorkers, a day of fun and sun. Even its hot dog became the biggest ever seen on the North American continent.

Eastern Long Island and Block Island

"Pudding Hill," Ocean Avenue, East Hampton. The name Pudding Hill is derived from a Revolutionary War incident in which the mistress of the eighteenth-century house on the site threw her newly cooked pudding down the hill at bothersome British soldiers.

The view from Ocean Dunes north across Hook Pond. Summer cottages, with their carriage houses and icehouses, lined the shore of Hook Pond in Southampton.

The coming of the railroad to Long Island in the 1830s in combination with the steamboat and stagecoach made possible summer travel to the remote eastern end. The rails reached from Brooklyn to Jamaica in 1836, to Hicksville in 1837, to Farmingdale in 1841, to Medford in early 1844, and to Greenport in July. Greenport was the last stop on the line. There passengers disembarked to take a ferry to Stonington, Connecticut, the fastest route to Boston in its day.

Meanwhile, the natives along the railroad were up in arms. Their livestock had been slaughtered by the iron machines and forest fires had frequently blazed up from the sparks flung out by the wood-burning engines. In retaliation ambushes against the railroad were frequent. In one instance a locomotive fell into the Peconic River after a party of natives sawed through timbers on the bridge. Throughout the 1850s

Ocean Avenue, East Hampton, 1900. Moving from foreground to background, dates are the stucco and half-timber gable house built in 1889; the gambrel-roof house built in 1890; the house with round towers built in 1899; the house with light-colored roof built in 1896; at the far end of the street, the cottage built in 1889.

Bathers by a rowboat, circa 1874. An unknown group out for a day of water and sun.

Long Islanders continued to resist the railroad, and Sunday trains were prohibited for awhile. However, the pressure for railroad profits and the influx of tourists eventually stilled the local outcry.

In mid-century the shores and islets of Long Island teemed with crabs, clams, oysters, and waterfowl, and the whole south shore of the island facing the Atlantic was a wonderful place for sportsmen and those fond of boating.

A few mid-century visitors braved the long journey by rail and stage to Montauk Point on the extreme eastern end of Long Island. Disturnell's 1855 guidebook noted:

There is a public house near by, much resorted to in the warm season, by strangers from every quarter. . . . There is a sublimity and a wildness, as well as solitariness here, which leaves a powerful impression on the heart. . . . On the extreme point, stands the tall white column, erected by the United States Government for a light-house, in 1795.

Montauk Point was still a wilderness in 1870 when Charles Parsons, a prominent New York artist and lithographer, took off from the city with a party of artists on a bright October afternoon. A pretty little steamer, the *Eastern City*, took them to Sag Harbor. The steamer threaded its way by Ravenswood and Astoria, on the right, and out into Flushing Bay, passing Riker's Island and Whitestone—the place of rendezvous for the New York Yacht Fleet. After leaving Fort Schuyler behind, with its heavy guns and battlements, the little steamer chugged

A United States Life-Saving Hut, circa 1876. Rudely constructed station huts were common sights along the Long Island coast from 1850 onward. The lifesaving dress, new in the 1870s, caused one observer to report having seen "some amphibious monster, deporting one moment in the water and next on land."

"Sommariva," an Italian villa on Jefferys Lane, East Hampton, designed by its owner, a civil engineer, and built in 1872.

into Long Island Sound. As twilight deepened, the lighthouse beacon at Sand's Point glowed in the distance and moonlight sparkled on the rippling water lending enchantment to the journey.

The next morning when the party awakened, the boat was already secured to the Sag Harbor dock and a stage stood waiting. It was decided to breakfast late at East Hampton and to then make a sketching tour of the ancient town. On the approach of East Hampton the forest along the roadside gave way to cultivated fields. The old church spire came into view and weatherbeaten old houses, set in deep foliage, were close to footpaths, and here and there were large flocks of geese "stretching in undulating lines across the road." In the distance the travelers caught a view of a picturesque windmill in gentle motion. After a leisurely breakfast the artists, complete with sketching materials, visited the birthplace of J. Howard Payne, celebrated author of "Home, Sweet Home."

Early the next morning the party began a long tramp to Montauk Point. Mile after mile the walk continued along the sea with occasional breaks for rest or for gathering beach plums. The walking gradually grew more difficult as the day wore on. For hours they had trudged over the "dreaded Napeague Beach," said by many to be impassable. Lifesaving stations were spaced at four-mile intervals with boats ready to launch, though in very heavy surf the boats were of no use. Gradually the broken, sandy dunes evolved into irregular bluffs. In early afternoon hospitality was offered to the group at the first house, where over a thousand head of horses and sheep grazed in nearby fields. After dinner the walk continued, following the coastline until Mr. Osborne's was reached after dark. The hotel was unusual in that patrons recounted their doings—a successful day's sport of wild game or stories of storms and shipwrecks. At bedtime the hostess asked for preferences of beds—feathers or straw. The preference was straw! Three snowy beds!

The hotel was near Fort Pond, an area well known to sportsmen. Looking east along the beach one could see a full half-mile of debris from wrecked ships, bringing to mind Walt Whitman's words, "The spasm of the sky and the shatter of the sea."

Toward noon of the next day a third house was reached, Stratton's, located on high ground with large numbers of cattle grazing on the hills. After dining on wild duck the party continued along the beach. Montauk Light was reached shortly after dark, the end of a tiring two-day hike. The keeper of the lighthouse took the travelers on a tour ascending the 137 steps to the tower, and the glorious panorama of moonlight on water was an inspiring sight.

After an early morning sketching session the party boarded a waiting team hired to take them to Greenport, from whence they would return by train to New York that evening.

With the opening up of Greenport to the railroad, Gardiner's Bay and vicinity with its multitude of beautiful islands became known by

The Satterthwaite Cottage, Ocean Avenue, East Hampton. Built in 1874 in what contemporaries called the Long Branch Style, today considered the Stick Style, this cottage was remodeled in the Colonial Revival style in 1894.

the early 1870s as a charming spot to visit. Few isolated places were so accessible. A steam ferry plied constantly between Greenport and Shelter Island Park. Also, a steamer line left New York every evening, landing guests at Shelter Island the following morning. Shelter Island, literally sheltered by islands, had many points and inlets. Most of the island's rich land was cultivated, having been settled from New England in about 1650. In 1873 it had some 700 inhabitants. Over the years the island became a sportsmen's paradise. Dering Harbor offered safe anchorage for yachts, and the waters of Gardiners and Peconic Bay were perfect for the sailing crowd.

The sea front of Locust Point, opposite Greenport, skirted a bluff twenty to fifty feet high. A charming spot, it had natural groves—oak, hickory, and cherry laced with grapevines and other trailing plants. On the highest point stood the Gothic four-story Manhasset House. The steamboat landing was reached from the hotel by an inclined concrete walk that sloped gradually down the ravine to the wharf. The spacious

Steamer Block Island, *circa 1875. For the tourist with a romantic penchant for lost treasure and unfound wrecks, Block Island was the place to go. The steamer was still running in the summer of 1898, leaving New London each weekday at quarter to ten via Watch Hill for a brief stop, and on to Block Island by twelve-thirty P.M.*

Block Island, Rhode Island, circa 1885. Private yachts and yachting clubs from Newport, Boston, and New York often set sail for Block Island, ten miles off the Rhode Island coast.

hotel had everything for comfort, including a barbershop and a billiard hall. The basement had a bakery, chill room, ice room, laundry, drying rooms, and also provided quarters for the servants.

The main line of the railroad had many branches by 1873, and a score of delightful, remote places became summer hideaways. The Sag Harbor Branch of the railroad ran to Quogue, a popular resort with several large boardinghouses. Sag Harbor was a prosperous village with several good hotels. Daily stages ran from Bridgehampton five miles from Sag Harbor to East Hampton, still in the later 1880s a quiet town, with bathing at nearby Napeague Beach. Montauk Point was still reached by private conveyance.

By the end of the century Long Island resorts remained small, with very few hotels of over 300 rooms. Summer towns catered to a quiet clientele or to sportsmen or yachting enthusiasts. The glamor of faraway places lured the more socially minded New Yorkers. When the Tile Club, a group of artists from New York, discussed in 1879 where to go on a proposed trip, only one member said Long Island, and because it was "not the place to go" the matter was settled—all agreed on a boating-sketching trip to Long Island!

Block Island, a place long known for its legends of shipwrecks, is only fifteen miles off the coast of Rhode Island. A steamer ran daily from Newport, and it could also be reached by steamer from Montauk Point. The island is picturesque, with hills and valleys, tiny ponds and springs, and two lovely lakes, one fresh, the other saltwater. At the northern extremity of the twenty-square-mile island stands the lighthouse—clay bluffs and white stretches of beach surround it, and the overall landscape is one of pastures, farmhouses, and the sea.

Near the island's only harbor, on its eastern side, was a tiny settlement of houses. Here was the center of activity in 1876—the fish houses, one large and one small hotel, and a sprinkling of boardinghouses, a handful of shops, a church, and two windmills—all appearing as though tossed there carelessly by the wind.

To the tourists' delight, a large eating establishment was a feature at the harbor—its owner, an ex-preacher, used the building for religious services on Sundays.

From the village many winding roads branched out in all directions, some to private dwellings secured by gates. All told there were thirteen hundred inhabitants in 1876—three-fourths of them farmers and the rest fishermen.

The Great Bathing Beach, a main attraction to tourists, is two miles long and considered as fine as anywhere along the Atlantic coast. The southern cliffs formed of clay, vivid with a variety of colors, are another attraction. One visitor wrote: "The profiles of the cliffs are both

Ocean View Hotel, Block Island, Rhode Island, circa 1874.

The Island lies nine leagues away.
Along its solitary shore,
Of craggy rock and sandy bay,
No sound but ocean's roar

Richard Henry Dana wrote a lengthy poem about Block Island in 1833, long before the natives had to share the island with summer tourists. In the 1870s the island was still a quiet place with only one large hotel (above). But not for long—by 1886 there were eighteen hotels with rooms for 2,500 people. When the electric trolley car was all the rage in 1892, the Block Islanders added horsecars for the visitors' convenience.

graceful and fantastic, and when looming against a glowing sky or out of a bank of fog, they are imposing to the last degree. . . . But to enjoy this cliff scenery in its perfection, you must look upon it under various aspects—in a wild storm . . . in a heavy fog . . . at sunset . . . at twilight . . . and in the moonlight."

Shipwrecks and the stories surrounding them were commonplace on the island. From 1856 to 1876 not less than sixty ships were lost on its shores; two lifesaving stations were built in the 1870s.

By 1898 the once primitive island was a full-blown summer resort offering boating, bathing, and fishing. Accommodations were also good —six hotels with 100 rooms each, three with 150 to 200 rooms each, one with 500 rooms, and sixteen others with smaller quarters.

Newport

Newport—elegant, quiet, fashionable, with the romance of soft sea air, picturesque scenery, and the flavor of history that only very old towns have. Aristocratic Newport, glittering with its fashionable summer visitors, became the showplace of the whole Atlantic coast, looked up to by the blue bloods of Europe. It was said that it was easier to become a member of European court circles than to join the gilded society of these multimillionaires from Boston and New York.

In early days southern families came to Newport for quiet summering, but when the Ocean House and Atlantic Hotel were built in 1840, quiet times were left behind. By 1844 polka lessons were being given in the surf. Guests whiled away the time with bowling, fishing, boating, driving to local places of interest, or walking along the famous cliffs, and the local Germania Musical Society played during hours designated for dancing or promenading.

The beach about a half mile from the hotel was the main attraction. A white flag hoisted over the bathhouses signalled the bathing hours, from nine o'clock until noon. Every morning, crowds of people poured out of the hotels, boardinghouses, and cottages, and horse teams raced along Bath Road to the beach, the carriage wheels crunching on the gravel road, then gliding silently on the smooth, hard sand. Soon the bevies of beauties emerged from the tiny bathhouses looking like "marine monsters." The bathing costumes were all colors: "such dresses—such patterns—such hats—such caps—and such an absence of starch and crinoline!" Near noon the carriages departed, the

A carriage ride on the beach, circa 1880.

*A summer portrait,
circa 1887.*

Mr. Andrew's Villa, circa 1872. Newport had many beautiful areas and Ochre Point, often called Millionaire's Point, was among them. The splendor of the villas there was said to surpass "the luxurious country seats of the Roman patricians."

Ocean House, circa 1870.

The Caretaker's Lodge, Pierre Lorillard Estate, circa 1874. All summerhouses in Newport, no matter how pretentious, were called cottages and Lorillard, an entrenched member of society and owner of a tobacco factory in Jersey City, went one better in calling his The Caretaker's Lodge.

white flag was pulled down, and up went a blood-red banner to signal that nude bathing was permitted until 3:00 P.M.. Servants and others had their prescribed bathing hours in the evening.

The more genteel days of hotel life must have faded by the mid-1850s, for the editor of *Harper's Monthly Magazine* complained: "There is not a good hotel in Newport; a clean and comfortable house, we mean, like that at Nahant . . . yet Newport is the great watering place of the country. . . . We humbly suggest that a good hotel upon the cliff, well organized and well-kept would draw the permanent summer population as well as the transitory visitors. And we say this, with all deference in proper quarters, not because our purse, but our stomach gave out." But when another voiced the view that Newport had begun to decline, his answer was, "The fickle tyrant of fashion can never reduce the sea-side retreat to the desolation of Ballston. . . . There will still be the sea, and the shore, and the wide solitary fields. There will still be the cliffs, and the rocks, and the inland hills . . . the lovely western bay . . . still the soft warm, sapphire ocean. . . ." Nevertheless, complaints continued to be heard. In 1858 social lions planning to go abroad for the summer were heard to say, "Go to Newport? A few miles of sand, a white wooden barn, very dirty, full of nothing to eat, and acres of tawdry dressed dowdies and tailor's-blocks?"

A lady visitor from Boston reported in 1865 that she found the busy promenade of men, women, and children with nurses, walking along the hotel piazza, fascinating. The men were laughing and agreeable, and the women wearing crisp white dresses flirted as outrageously as young girls. Young ladies paraded by in groups, wearing high heels with their dresses hitched up to show big rosettes and ruffled petticoats—their hair stuffed out in waterfalls as big as "a peddler's pack behind their backs." Bathing costumes at the beach were described as "queer-looking Bloomer suits . . . and great broad-brimmed hats." Women too weak at home to pick up a handkerchief stood the brunt of the breakers and swam around like mermaids.

Driving in the afternoon, especially along Bellevue Avenue and past the Ocean House, was the thing to do. it was reported that the newly rich aped foreign aristocracy, driving about in barouches with drivers and footmen in gold lace and livery, the black drivers wearing white kid gloves and rosettes on the sides of their tall hats. They did indeed look like royalty, with their plumes, gaily colored shawls, scarlet opera capes, diamonds, and lace.

In 1874 the town already had about five hundred cottages and villas, of which about two hundred were rented each season at fabulous prices, from two to eight thousand dollars. A fashionable villa with grounds cost anywhere from fifty thousand to two hundred thousand dollars. The most exclusive residences were on Bellevue Avenue to Bath Road, Cliff Walk, Touro Street, and Narragansett Avenue. Landscape

The Cliffs, circa 1865. Everyone liked to wander up along the two-mile cliff walk, just south of the beach with the splendid vista of the sea on one side and the cottages of Newport, with their lush green lawns and colorful gardens, on the other.

The home of Mrs. Sturdivant Fish, circa 1900, above. The stately homes of Newport were a backdrop to the simple pleasures of walking, bathing, driving along First Beach, or strolling along Cliff Walk, overlooking the sea.

Cliff Villas, circa 1872. It was said in the 1870s that "a summer residence in Newport has grown to be a luxury forbidden to many." The average rate to rent a villa for the season was from $3,000 to $4,000, including the services of a gardener. Newport boasted many expensive shops and a plumbing service only the rich could afford.

artists created beautiful terraces, conservatories, fishponds, arbors, summer houses, and gardens glowing with brilliant color. Staying at a hotel was no longer fashionable, and society revolved about the activities of the villa colony.

The most fashionable afternoon outing was to Fort Adams, where late in the afternoon the band played for a few hours and the smart set listened and exchanged pleasantries.

One of the most beautiful drives was along Bath Road past the First Beach to Purgatory Bluffs and the Second Beach (Sachuest Beach), where hanging rocks skirted part of the sand. Farther along the drive, on the eastern shore of the island, was a delightful wooded area called the Glen or Lover's Retreat. And nearby was the famous Mrs. Durfee's Tea House of the Glen.

> And then, when our lovely Glen Ramble is past,
> And we rest our tired limbs on a sofa at last,
> How delightful to mark on the table outspread
> The primrose-hued butter, the delicate bread!
> The cakes and the cream, the preserves and the ham,
> The eggs, the hung beef, the sliced peaches and jam,
> The coffee so fragrant, the fine flavored tea,
> And the other good things of good Mrs. Durfee!

The summer population in the 1880s, five thousand at most, centered about two exclusive clubs, the Newport and the Casino. The smart set retreated still farther, visiting among themselves and having teas and dinners cooked by French chefs. But they still played polo and

Vigilant and Valkyrie II, *racing, 1893.*
"October 13th, in a rattling easterly breeze
and a choppy sea, the Vigilant *finished her*
task by beating the Valkyrie *in the finest*
yacht race ever sailed in American
waters."

Polo game, Newport.

went to the Casino for weekly concerts and dances, and society never failed to attend the annual lawn tennis tournaments.

American yachting was at its zenith in Newport, for many of the owners of famous yachts lived there. The New York Yacht Club, the oldest in the country, made an annual rendezvous at Newport. Throughout the summer the harbor became a sea of mast and sail. When night fell, Chinese lanterns lit the harbor, their soft, swaying colors reflected in the water. When the yachting crowd from Newport went looking for a day of fun, they often sailed over to Narragansett Pier. Everyone bathed, and spectators sat in red-lined straw chairs or in little tents on the sand and went on to the attractive casino for lunch.

By the nineties people of modest means began to summer in Newport. The beautiful drives, once exclusive, were infiltrated by "mammoth loads of excursionists" curious to see the palatial mansions and beautifully landscaped grounds they read about in the Sunday papers. They came from Providence and Pawtucket bringing bag lunches, peanuts, and soda pop—they took over the town squares, cliffs, and beach. No longer was there a set bathing hour. Society did not mingle with the ordinary bathers; the watchers in carriages no longer came onto the beach. The beach was crowded on Sundays with excursionists and off-duty servants. The travelling photographer set up his shanty. Pavilions similar to those on Coney Island were built, pervaded by the aroma of chowder.

A walk on the cliffs, from Our Native Land, *1891.*

The activities of the Coaching Club were reported by the Newport Mercury *in 1893: "The spot chosen for the meet was an ideal one and the whole affair from start to finish was a complete success. There were nine coaches in line, and drawn by the beautiful horses, driven by their owners in their brilliant green driving coats, yellow waistcoats and high silk hats, and freighted with charming ladies in dainty costumes, the line made a very pretty picture as it wended its way to the Golf Club grounds, via Ochre Point, Bellevue and Ocean Avenues."*

"The line was formed on Narragansett avenue, corner of Bellevue avenue, and moved at 12:45, going to Bateman's where Caterer Bussell of the Casino had an elaborate luncheon served . . . a large crimson tent [was] erected for the purpose by Col. A. C. Landers."

Martha's Vineyard

It was the Methodists who discovered how delightful the island of Martha's Vineyard could be in the warm days of August when camp-meeting time came around. In 1835 the devout came from mainland towns or neighboring islands to spend a week of prayer. Who minded sleeping in tents on beds of straw when the nights were cooled by sea breezes and the air was fragrant with flowering bushes? The Methodist group leased a beautiful tract of land with old oak trees and a pond for their yearly meetings and called it Wesleyan Grove. Large tents housed the brethren. Rules for the camp-meeting site were strict: anyone hawking, peddling, giving shows or plays or engaged in gambling or horse racing was subject to a twenty-dollar fine. Tenting in the lovely grove was so pleasurable that more people came every year, and some began to put up their tents before camp meeting and stayed on after.

By 1853 the campgrounds took on the appearance of a snow-white city—160 tents were pitched, and on the big day of the meeting 4,000 people came to worship. With many coming in by steamer from the mainland, complaints began that a few of the "baser sort" had crept in:

"Groups of evil-minded strangers who may come to take up quarters in the neighboring woods, to revel with their bottles, are very likely to be detected, or to have their hidden treasures found and *cared for,* still some do, occasionally, try to see how well they can elude the vigilance of officers of the meeting. At this time, some fifteen bottles, well filled, were found snugly nested in the woods, and on the morning of the close were brought out and disposed of according to their demerits."

Large tents were soon put to use as boarding tents where wholesome food was served. With steamboat excursions and special trains bringing in visitors by the thousands, Martha's Vineyard camp meeting had become the largest in the world—12,000 came for the big Sunday in August 1859.

Oak Bluffs Landing, circa 1872. The steamers Monohansett *and* Martha's Vineyard *plied a summertime run between New Bedford, Oak Bluffs, and Katama. Visitors recalled the trip as pleasant and picturesque, with the clank of the walking beam and the whirl of the big wheels slapping the water. Vacationers could stroll along the beach by Vineyard Sound and enjoy the pleasant sea breeze and the excitement of the steamer docking.*

Cottages on Clinton Avenue camp-
grounds, circa 1872. In 1859 cottages
began to replace tents on the campgrounds.
The buildings, which were privately owned,
were put up on land leased from the
Association. Some of these tiny Gothic
cottages were modeled after tents, their
wide doorways left open to catch the breezes.

Sea View Avenue, Oak Bluffs, circa 1874. There were many elegant houses built on Sea View Avenue in the late 1800s. The landmark of Oak Bluffs and the finest hotel in the new resort was the Sea View House, which stood at the head of the wharf in the new harbor. Visitors could choose from a number of small hotels and boardinghouses in Oak Bluffs for less expensive accommodations. The small hotels charged $2 a day for transients and from $10 to $12 weekly for permanent lodgers. Boardinghouses charged slightly less—$8 to $10 per week.

Close-up of Sea View Avenue, circa 1884. Parades, band concerts, and fireworks displays could be seen from the wide front porches of the Sea View Avenue houses. The concrete avenues paved by the Oak Bluffs land company were ideal for tricycling.

In the 1860s, hated worldliness had definitely arrived. By 1866 bathhouses, boats, and even a tintype saloon appeared on the landscape. The time was ripe for a new resort to develop. The land next to the camp-meeting tract, including the acreage between the campgrounds and the shores known as the Great Pasture, was purchased by the Oak Bluffs Land and Wharf Company, which began advertising the new resort as "homes by the seaside." One thousand lots were offered for sale at $100 each (by 1873 they went for $1,600). A Boston landscape gardener was called in to lay out the town with streets, parks, lots, and a wharf.

Harper's Weekly in 1868 wrote: "They play croquet. Just below the steamboat landing there is a beach for bathing . . . when evening sets in the girls put away their croquet and attend to the tea-making; then comes the evening service around the cottage doors, while outside the young people are promenading in the gaily lighted streets of the improvised village." Meanwhile, the camp-meeting people were up in arms and built a seven-foot-high picket fence around their grounds to keep out these worldly affairs.

By 1870 the land company owned three small hotels, the wharf, bathhouses, fire engines, and a police office. Plans went ahead to build the huge Sea View Hotel at the head of the wharf. These were the magic days. Bands played at the wharf as boats arrived. The new resort soon became known as the cottage city of America; by 1873, 691 charming Gothic-style cottages had been built and the paved streets of the spanking-new town were illuminated by gaslights. Horse railroads, a trotting

Governor Sprague's Cottage, circa 1872. The former governor of Rhode Island, William Sprague, owned this cottage on the island.

course, and a narrow-gauge railroad soon followed, running along the shore and linking Oak Bluffs by way of Edgartown to the new resort of Katama. The train was wonderful for sightseeing, and though the railroad later failed, it did much to fan the fires of the building boom during the 1870s.

Meanwhile, back in 1869, the Camp Meeting Association formed a land company of its own, the Vineyard Grove Company. They purchased fifty-five acres on the far side of the pond beyond the campground and began building houses, calling the new development Vineyard Highlands. In 1872 the company built Highland House, a sixty-room hotel on the seaside, as well as a new steamboat landing and a plank road leading to the meeting grounds. The new road became a fashionable promenade for visitors to the Highlands. The new resort must have had a religious tone, because a Baptist group bought property there in 1875 and built a wooden church, bringing in material from a Philadelphia Centennial building. Lots were sold with strict rules outlawing liquor and gambling.

The most successful resort on Martha's Vineyard, other than Oak Bluffs was Katama, planned by some of the same promoters as at Oak Bluffs. Katama had a good harbor on the bay, making it a fine place for yachting and fishing. A hotel, Mattakeset Lodge, went up on a high bluff at the end of the harbor, appealing especially to lovers of the sea,

View near Preacher's Stand campgrounds, circa 1868. Until 1870 camp meetings were held in the open air. When the meetings were not in session, the park was used for pleasurable pursuits; mothers aired their babies and young people gathered under the oak trees near the preacher's stand. In 1870 the Camp Meeting Association brought in a great Tabernacle tent to shelter the worshipers and the clergy.

The Tabernacle tent is said to have been made like a circus tent of four thousand yards of sailcloth sewed together in six sections. The Methodists replaced the canvas tent with an iron tabernacle, dedicated in 1879. The ubiquitous President Grant attended a prayer meeting here on Big Sunday in August of 1874.

Saloon in Wesley Grove, Oak Bluffs, circa 1875. Although Martha's Vineyard was not a "dry" island, the Camp Meeting Association frowned on drinking. However, "Ottawa Beer" seems to have been popular with the resorters!

with its balconies and broad verandas. Its entire upper story was devoted to a gallery, where delightful sea breezes cooled promenaders and dancers every evening. Success was assured for the new venture when the citizens of Edgartown laid out and built a beautiful twelve-mile drive connecting Katama to the town of Vineyard Haven via Edgartown and Oak Bluffs. Sea View Boulevard, as it was called, ran along the sea and past beautiful lakes. Along the drive a few miles from Oak Bluffs was a deep channel spanned by a bridge where fishing enthusiasts of all ages caught bluefish, bass, and flounder.

Cottage City in the 1880s and 1890s catered to fashion—bands played at the wharf when the boats came in, but the sparkle had gone. The Oak Bluffs Land and Wharf Company was in trouble. Many of the old hotels were destroyed by fire, including the landmark Sea View House in 1892 and the Highland House in 1894. An old era had gone and a new one would begin.

Nantucket

Old House, circa 1878. One of the great attractions for summer visitors was this ancient house, built in 1686. Its shingled sides and small-paned windows marked an earlier age.

Summer on the sands, opposite. "They are so intent, so full of life, who out of sun and sea, are building dream fantasies of sand while the rapid hours pass." Once the scene of bustling activity during its glorious whaling days, Nantucket became a haven for tourists in the late 1800s.

Those who wanted to escape to an earlier age chose the old whaling town of Nantucket. The tourist of the 1870s could take a morning train from Boston to Hyannis on Cape Cod and from there board the steamer *Island Home* for the three-hour sail to the island. He could expect quite a welcoming committee when the boat docked: most of the town's population turned out to look the passengers over and to get their mail and gossip from the outside world.

At the wharf a great variety of vehicles was waiting to transport passengers. It was a surprise to the first-time visitor to see that most of the waiting wagons were old-fashioned Nantucket carts with two wheels, steps in the rear, and no permanent seats—often just kitchen chairs to sit on. The story ran that native lads liked to take girls out in these "jaunting carts" and slyly unfasten the cart hooks at an opportune moment, causing the squealing girls to slide out onto the soft sand. The more modern carts had four wheels and resembled coal wagons, with high sides that gave protection from winter winds but blocked the view of the summer visitor. If he looked around, the fashionable visitor could find a "regular" hack to take him to the hotel.

After the visitor settled down at comfortable quarters in town, he was again taken back to old times—a town crier with his bell made rounds three times a day to announce lectures, meetings, and new arrivals, a custom still going strong in the 1870s. A walk about town gave the tourist a feeling of the old whaling days when Nantucket had been a bustling, wealthy community. Many of the very old houses still stood, some with widows' walks on the roofs from which to watch the weather and the return of sailing craft. The one active business street was near the water, where at the proper hour the old fish dealers, their seafaring days over, sat telling strange sea tales to all who would listen. Farther up the street tourists and natives alike congregated at the auctions, where curious old things were offered.

Bathing at Nantucket. "Bathing costumes at Nantucket are as charming as they can be made, and some of the boldest swimmers are seen here beyond the rollers."

The Springfield House, 1888. The hospitable Springfield House on North Water Street was one of the larger hotels in Nantucket, with accommodations for two hundred guests.

The last whaling ship sailed in 1869 and Nantucket turned to tourism for a living. The town was fortunate in having a glistening white beach and excellent bathing close by. It was said of the bathing beach, "Safety, quiet, and delicious temperature—nowhere can they be found in greater perfection." Not far out of town the artist Eastman Johnson summered in his house perched on a cliff above the beach, using a second house as a studio.

Everyone coming to Nantucket made the drive to the small village of Siasconset at the tip of the island. The road was one track and deeply rutted. The land was "scantily clothed with grass, weeds, and low shrubs, and totally destitute of both trees and enclosure." Early settlers had cut down most of the trees. An 1855 guidebook told about Siasconset.

"It consists of a hotel and a number of boardinghouses, which are thronged during the summer by invalids and pleasure-seeking tourists. The eastern extremity of the island terminates in a bluff, perhaps sixty feet in height. The top of the bluff is a smooth plain of the greenest verdure. Here about a hundred cottages, of Lilliputian dimensions, have been erected . . . and are occupied by the more wealthy inhabitants of Nantucket . . . in the middle of the summer. . . . Most of these houses . . . cost from three to five hundred dollars. . . . From this bluff you look down upon the far extending beach. . . ."

A magnificent view of the island, near Siasconset, was described by the historian John Barber in 1839.

"From a neighboring eminence, called *Sancoty Head,* the eye commands almost the entire horizon. The rich coloring of the sky, reflected by the distant water, the distinct outline of the town of Nantucket with its steeples and busy wind-mills, the repose of the surrounding plains, contrasted with the gloom which broods over the rolling and roaring ocean in the rear, give rise to sensations which can be felt but not described."

Group in bathing dress, circa 1890.

By the mid-1870s Nantucket was coming to the fore as a watering place. Invalids came for quiet and repose, and rugged sport fishermen came for the thrill of shark fishing in rough waters. It was a wonderful place for boating and fishing, and the seafaring men of the island made perfect guides. The town had such attractions as an atheneum, a library, marine curiosities, and ancient houses of historic interest. By the end of the century, the island had gained quite a reputation for entertaining visitors in its own little world.

Bostonian Retreats

"Sprinkle, now, the sea with sails, the land with cottages and groves, the marshes with mounds of yellow hay; fix a lighthouse on this island or that headland; put a collar of foam about yonder isolated rock, a fringe of white surf on the hem of the sea . . ." So was Cape Ann described by a visitor in 1878.

When summer heat hovered over Boston, its citizens could find relief at the many delightful breeze-swept nooks and crannies along the Massachusetts Bay coast. Spots along the coast, dormant for years, became by the 1870s beehives of activity during the summer. New hotels, boardinghouses, modest cottages, and costly new villas gave the old coastal towns a new look.

The North Shore, beginning about ten miles north of Boston and continuing up to the tip of Cape Ann, was a paradise for well-to-do Boston businessmen who commuted daily to their summer homes by boat or rail. Life along the North Shore was dull compared to fashionable resorts, but it was well suited to conservative Bostonians. Elaborate balls and lavish entertaining were almost unheard of except at some of the summer hotels catering to short-time visitors.

A thirty-one-mile run on the railroad, from Boston to Gloucester, made it easy to reach many of the old towns and new resorts. Ten miles from Boston by rail was Swampscott, a suburb of Lynn, the favorite summer resort of many wealthy Bostonians. Its several hotels were always crowded. The town had a beautiful seaside drive said to be second only to the famous drive at Newport with magnificent ocean views. One of the quaint places of local interest was King's Beach, the haunt of lobstermen, their fishing shanties and boats leaning crookedly along the shore. A little farther along was Whale's Beach and the busy fish stalls, gaily decorated with names like *Laughing Water* and *Florence Nightingale*, where the local fishermen sold their catches.

Nahant had been a star sharing its light with Saratoga Springs as early as the 1820s. John Barber wrote in 1839: "Nahant is much visited.

Bathing House, Pigeon Cove, Cape Ann, circa 1875. Resort land speculation was booming in the 1870s, and the easy terms of real estate on the prestigious avenues of Cape Ann attracted many wise investors. After a ten-mile steamer ride of cards and gossip, the Boston businessman could enjoy an evening on Cape Ann, and there were beaches with modern bathing facilities for his vacationing family.

Formal gardens, Boston, 1872. Boston, like New York, was a stopover town. If a tourist liked to sightsee in Boston, he could gaze on the wonders of colonial America. And wandering to the byroads, he might chance upon a formal garden and recall an Englishman's words, "It looks like a good old English town."

Singer's Rock, Pigeon Cove, Cape Ann, circa 1871. "The great point of interest here is Pigeon Cove, situated about two miles from the railroad station. The highlands are now called 'Ocean View.' The fishing and bathing are fine, and the fame of the place has spread far and wide. The massive rocks form fine artistic and geological studies. Houses of entertainment abound in the vicinity, and private enterprise is doing much to adorn the situation."

Two steamboats are constantly running from Boston during the pleasant season, but a ride by land, over the beaches, is much more delightful. A spacious and elegant hotel has been erected of stone near the eastern extremity. It contains nearly a hundred rooms, and is surrounded by a double piazza. . . . Several other hotels and boarding houses are situated in the village. . . ." A visiting Englishman wrote in 1841 of watching fireflies on warm evenings, and told of icemen coming to every house in the mornings. Pineapples were sold in the streets from wheelbarrows for a shilling.

The sparkle of Nahant as a mecca for fashionable people dimmed by the fifties. A journalist wrote wistfully:

"You encounter no crowds of carriages or of curious and gossiping people. No fast men in velvet coats are trotting fast horses. The evenings at Nahant have a strange fascination. There are no balls, no

All aboard for Quisset, July 3, 1897. The *Vigilant Falmouth* and passengers. Gertrude Stein is in the last row, on the right.

Little girl and dog, tintype, circa 1875.

Quisset, July 3, 1897. Gertrude Stein and Radcliffe and Harvard friends in Quisset Harbor. A few members of the party appear to be foraging for clams, or perhaps mussels or oysters—all plentiful in the shallows.

Boston Harbor and East Boston from State Street, 1863. At Boston, travelers could take the luxury steamers of the Eastern Steamship Line to Maine or the Eastern Railroad to summer spots throughout the East.

Lynn Beach, circa 1870. Lynn was the stopping-off point for the North Shore. Also, the town had something that few summer visitors could resist—the lure of hidden treasure. It all began back in 1852, when Hiram Marble received directions from spirits to drill Dungeon Rock, a venture that proved unsuccessful, despite a 135-foot excavation Marble left when he died in 1868. However, his son did strike it rich—he charged twenty-five cents a head for an eerie walk through the cavern with a guide who believed in spirits.

hops, no concerts, no congregating under any pretense in hotel parlors. The damp night air is still, or throbs with the beating sea. The Nahanters sit upon their piazzas and watch the distant lighthouse or the gleam of a lantern upon a sail. Gradually they retire."

In an effort to turn the clock back to better days, a two-hundred-room hotel was built in 1854 to attract out-of-state people. Things appeared to brighten with the well-run hotel, but it was destroyed by fire seven years later and the grounds were bought up by those who preferred not to have their beautiful villas overrun by hotel guests.

In the 1870s several steamers a day brought multitudes of people to the Nahant peninsula to picnic on the beaches or to lunch and fish among the rocks, to the discomfort of the villa owners. One of the big attractions for the day excursionist was a picnic under the trees at Maolis Gardens. The management even had two lazy tame bears, whose awkward gambols delighted the children.

Anyone visiting Nahant was certain to hear many stories about sea monsters. Early in the century a sea snake was seen in the water off Nahant and a reward was offered for the serpent dead or alive. Vessels were fitted out by expert whalemen hopeful of catching the monster; nets were spread out in its known haunts. One adventuresome fellow said he had been close enough to see "the white of his glittering eye," and said he shot the contents of his gun into the monster's head.

Atlantic House, Nantasket, August 1881.
"Sailing and fishing are without limit; and
tens of thousands flock to enjoy the varied
beauties of the scene, and the soothing
temperature of the coast and sea air, when
the heated term is in full power."

However, the sea serpent eluded his pursuers and "shook the spray of Nahant Bay from his tail ere he disappeared in the depth of the ocean."

The old town of Marblehead, a few miles north, had clusters of quaint, small, wooden houses and narrow streets dating back to the Revolution. Into the harbor came yachts of every size. In the 1890s, when fashionable yachts came in from New York to the Eastern Yacht Club, the harbor would be aglow with electric lights and colored lanterns. Out on Marblehead Neck during the summer months the white tents of camping parties dotted the landscape. Fashionable Beverly Shores, with its magnificent big estates and plush villas, developed into a resort in the 1870s—a rich man's playground for horseback riding, hunting, and yachting. In the 1890s the local Myopia Hunt Club at Wenham sponsored polo three afternoons a week. The club also held fox hunts in the English red coat, hound, and horn tradition, galloping through nearby cornfields. At first the farmers condemned the sport as Anglomania, but after money had changed hands they relented and enjoyed the pomp and excitement. A good-will dance was given them each fall.

The prettiest area along the North Shore was in and around the region of Cape Ann, "flowery dells and wandering brooks, orchards, meadows, and fields of golden grain and with all of this a picturesque tract of woodland," the end of the line by rail. The nearest towns were

Pigeon Cove, circa 1869. There were many places to explore on Cape Ann. After doing Great Gully at Pigeon Cove, there still remained Swallows Cave, Irene's Grotto, Spouting Horn, Castle Rock, and many other spots.

Great Gully, Pigeon Cove, circa 1874.

Nahant, 1876, opposite. In the 1870s Nahant was a summer colony of villas and cottages. The innkeeping fraternity had long since given up trying to re-create the celebrated watering place of the 1830s. Come summertime, artists roamed the beaches setting up their easels in the shade of the rugged cliffs.

Gloucester and Rockport. A delightful resort called Bass Rock was located in East Gloucester. Cottage dwellers here had a fine marine view of outlying islands, a lighthouse, and, best of all, a broad, hard-packed beach wonderful for driving or bathing.

The village of Pigeon Cove with its granite hills and woods lay two miles beyond Rockport. Hundreds of narrow, winding footpaths led to the many rocky coves and inlets along the shore. Rock hunters found hordes of specimens to bring home. Pigeon Cove House and the Ocean View Hotel were the favorite hotels. Bordering the rocky shore at the extreme end of Cape Ann was a fifty-acre settlement laid out in the 1870s, considered by many to be the most desirable location along the entire New England coast. The resort had nicely graded avenues and walks fragrant with ferns, bayberry shrubs, and wild roses. One of the pleasant walks from Pigeon Cove led to the breakwater by the harbor, where visitors could view the wharves busy with fishermen and boatmen loading granite for shipment to Boston.

Each little resort had its own historical heritage. At Cohasset, lovers of nature could enjoy the wild beauty of the rocks where many ships had been wrecked off the town's coast during storms. The little town of Marshfield had been the home of Daniel Webster, and the railroad terminated at the town of Duxbury, founded by Captain Miles Standish.

The ultimate historic place for a day's outing was the famous relic of old Pilgrim days, Plymouth Rock, the American mecca, where "upward of fifty thousand persons come . . . every summer . . . making reverent pilgraimages to the cradle of American civilization."

The Russell House, Old Orchard Beach,
circa 1874.

A drug and knickknack store, Maine, circa
1885. Tourists found Maine stores plain
and direct—very different from the
glittering resort shops found elsewhere. If
a "rusticator" (as the natives called the
summer people) needed more, Portland
was the place to go—from there on out, it
was all vacation!

"The Travelers," tintype, circa 1876,
opposite. Train time was when the natives
turned out to see what the new crop of
vacationers looked like. These gentlemen
could easily have arrived on the busy
Boston and Maine.

Down East

"Leave Long Branch, and Newport, and Cape May, and the score
of high-sounding city-spoiled places . . . where Fashion holds high
carnival . . . leave all these, and flying Eastward, find at the Maine
coast such comforts, such scenery, and such surroundings as well make
your heart leap for joy. . . ."

In Maine, the last frontier for vacationers, the crowds were thinner,
the scenery unspoiled, the beaches splendid, and the coastal areas
steeped in old legends and traditions.

For the tourist travelling northeastward by rail or boat, Portland
was the threshold to Maine. Perched on hills, it had routes radiating by
road, railroad, or sea to many places of interest.

The famous Old Orchard Beach, with its numerous big wooden
hotels was but a half hour's ride to the south by train. The beach,
stretching nine miles from Pine Point to the Saco River, was smooth
and hard. At high tide two carriages could ride abreast, and at low tide
it was five to six hundred feet wide. Bathers were safe from the
dangerous undercurrents so feared in ocean bathing. For generations
native people came to Old Orchard Beach on June 26, following the
custom of the first English settlers, who believed the ocean had special
healing powers on that day. Thousands came: the old to be rejuvenated,
the middle-aged to be made stronger, and children and babies to be
"dipped" as protection against disease and death.

In 1873 the Methodists founded a camp-meeting site about half a
mile from Old Orchard Beach. They built a large amphitheatre to hold
seven thousand people, and soon a little city with neatly laid out
avenues and small cottages grew up. In the late eighties a horsecar
railroad began operating from Old Orchard to Saco and Biddeford.
"Beyond the campground the horse-cars run through a beautiful
country, the road on either side being lined with groves of hard woods
and evergreen."

For those who preferred carriage drives, picturesque highways
branched out from Old Orchard. One visitor wrote that "hedges are

A clambake, circa 1877, right. Land promotion sales drew their big crowds with free offerings. Along the seacoast, clambakes were always a surefire way to get into the spirit of things. Corn on the cob, potatoes, bluefish, clams, and crabs were roasted over red-hot stones, covered with seaweed. To round off the feasts, hot coffee, tea, rolls, bread-and-butter pickles, crackers, and other delicacies were served under the shade of a tent. Once the crowd was fed and in a festive mood, the sale began.

Three girls on the beach, circa 1878. Building sand castles, finding shells or bits of treasure—hours gone by that no clock could measure.

bright with the fragrant wild rose and bayberry, and as the summer declines the golden-rod and purple aster appear."

Farther south, down at Cape Arundel, Kennebunkport with its beautiful river and harbor was having a real-estate boom in 1873. A branch line of the Boston & Maine Railroad brought it to within a short drive of the Orchard Beach Station. Land speculators (the Boston and Kennebunkport Seashore Company) bought up a tract of seven hundred acres including seven miles of seacoast, and landscape gardeners were brought in to beautify the grounds. The many old farmhouses in the tract were patched and painted and soon filled to overflowing with summer boarders. A hotel went up and lots were sold quickly to "persons of culture and taste." Appealing to romantics were the moonlight excursions on the Kennebunk River.

The summer tourist leaving Portland for the north took a boat or train to Bath and from there traveled by stagecoach or small boat to the resort of Boothbay Harbor. In the 1850s Boothbay was a favorite place

Camp life in the Maine woods, 1885. Away from the dwellings of men, deep in the wilds of the Maine woods, northeast of Moosehead Lake, came this party of rugged explorers in the summer of 1885.

for bathing, sailing, shooting, and fishing. By 1883 the town's two small hotels were "overflowing with summer guests, who clamber about the crooked hill-streets, and among the gray old wharves, and sail up and down the harbor, and among the islands beyond."

Far out at sea, the one-thousand-acre island of Monhegan was a little Methodist hamlet in 1883. Summer visitors coming by sailboat from Boothbay stayed at Mrs. Albee's boardinghouse.

Farther up the coast was the little city of Belfast, with its old gray wharves and old-fashioned business streets—a fine old seacoast city from which to make excursions. Steamboats left every day for the farther reaches of Penobscot Bay, and stages left for many outlying towns. The Methodists founded Wesleyan Grove near Belfast, and the camp-meeting ground became a summer port for bay steamers. A delightful bay breeze swept over the camp city, cooling the many summer cottages and hotels snuggled among the groves. The summit of Mount Percival, with a fine view of the bay and open sea, was only a mile by good carriage road from the campgrounds.

Bar Harbor

"At Rodick's," 1883.

ar Harbor, the last of the ultraexclusive resorts of the North Atlantic coast, was founded on the wonderful island of Mount Desert. Forests, lakes and ponds, mountains and glens, sounds and the bay, beaches and rugged rocks, and the panorama of the open sea were all bound together in the one hundred square miles of the island. "The perfect sapphire of the sea reflects the overarching sky, and is framed by gray and pink and brown cliffs, light-green meadow-lands, silvery beaches, and surging leagues of dark forest."

The earliest summer visitors to the town of Bar Harbor were artists with an eye for beauty but little money. The simplicity of the island changed rapidly when fashionable visitors discovered the place. It soon became an elite resort, especially for upper-crust Bostonians. Steamboats began service to the resort in 1868, and by 1870 fourteen hotels had been built at Bar Harbor. In 1855 the Agamont Hotel and a few farmhouses were the only buildings in town.

Life at the hotels in the 1870s was high-spirited and full of youthful gaiety. Most summer guests seemed to be under twenty-five, which made it a good place for society matchmaking. Rodick's Hotel, the most popular in town, had lively young men in flannels and knickerbockers and pretty girls in feminine finery who made the hotel's "hops" a favorite excuse for gathering. "The famous 'fish-pond' at Rodick's was a large hall in which the young people used to assemble after breakfast and the early dinner, and in which the girls were supposed to angle for their escorts. Some of the prettiest girls in the country were gathered together there, and the soft vowels of the South mingled with the decided consonants of the Westerner." Daytime fun was gathering on buckboards for a large picnic and on Eagle Lake, where canoes and rowboats could be hired.

In the early evenings the harbor was crowded with boats and canoes; spectators sat on rocks along the shore. As it got dark the boats began coming in one by one. Many of the couples, their appetites

The Ovens, Mt. Desert, 1883. Tuesday, August 7. *"Thence to Handcock Point and across to the Ovens, where we hailed George and Miss Horning and Miss Ellen who had driven up from Bar Harbor. . . ."*

Rodick's Hotel, 1883. One of the three best hotels in Bar Harbor.

sharpened by the sea air, had supper parties at Sproul's Restaurant or at the small tavern which served drinks in defiance of the state prohibition law.

Hotel life was at its zenith when socialite Frances Tracy Morgan and her famous husband J. P. Morgan visited Rodick's Hotel in 1875. It was during these years that a great many yachts began visiting Bar Harbor. The navy too began to pay regular visits to the resort, the officers socializing with affluent cottagers, much to the delight of the young ladies.

From about 1880 more and more millionaries and others of the Boston elite began coming to Bar Harbor, buying up land and building imposing villas and estates hidden from view by lush, beautifully kept grounds. The larger hotels were forced out of business and the local people became servants of the manor lords. Money was king, and soon the town had all the modern improvements: a fire department, a pure water system, and sewers.

The quiet barons of the island sat in their palatial homes while their vassals went about town with an air of cheerful informality. Sightseers were tolerated, but there was little doubt that Bar Harbor had become a millionaire's colony.

Henry Pettit's Album

August, 1883

Henry Pettit. The diarist (foreground) enjoys a quiet moment in Maine with his friends.

Thursday, Aug. 2/83. Left *Philadelphia* by 1:30 P.M. train from Broad St. Station, for *New York.* In company with Miss Martha M. Horning of Philada. and Mr. George W. Bacon. At Jersey City took the Brooklyn Annex Boat, which after a circuitous route around the battery and stoppage at East End of the Bridge in Brooklyn, brought us back to the pier of the Fall River Line in New York. There were joined by Miss Ellen M. Wood of Mt. Kisco, N.Y., who had arrived during the morning to become one of the "tourists." Left at 5:30 P.M.

Bar Harbor from the water, 1883.
Saturday, August 4. *"Arrived at Bar Harbor at about 2 p.m. and were met at the wharf by Miss Dolly and Miss Emily Warder and their uncle, Mr. Price...."*

upon the new Steamer *Pilgrim* of the Fall River Line of Sound Boats. Had excellent state rooms upon the outer side, upper deck. As usual enjoyed the scenery along the East river, and the excellent orchestra in the saloon during the evenings. Noticed particularly the late introduction of the electric lights (Edison's) into the state rooms, also in exposed places upon the outer deck. The style of decoration of this new palace steamer shows a reaction for the better from the more brilliant and gaudy ornamentation which has been in vogue of recent years upon boats of that class. The introduction of the bay wood (mahogany) and absence of extra gilding was a good sign of a more subdued popular taste.

Friday, Aug. 3. Arrived at the *Old Colony Depot, Boston.* Drove to the *Boston and Maine Depot.* Took breakfast and left at 9 A.M. for *Portland.* Enjoyed first breath of sea air, fresh from the breakers, as we passed *Old Orchard Beach.* Found the *Falmouth hotel* in Portland only passably satisfactory. Took a walk upon the bluffs, and later all the party drove around the city, greatly enjoying the superb views of

the famous sea port, the harbor, distant White Mts. in N.H., etc., also noticed the exceptionally comfortable and refined aspects of many of the dwellings of the city, surrounded by stately elms and shrubbery, well-kept lawns, and not a few new buildings which showed that the community is more thoroughly in rapport with the latest best architectural work of the day.

At about 9 P.M. went on board our steamer, the *Lewiston,* for the north—sailed at 11 P.M., upon arrival of the express train from Boston. Rather too dark to see much as we passed out of the harbor, except by star-light, but the winding course of the steamer, and the dark massive outline of White Head Bluff on Cushing's Island, which came out in relief even in the darkness of the landscape.

Saturday, Aug. 4. Say 6 A.M., we were in the harbor of *Rockland* when I went on deck. Took on passengers who had come by night train from Boston. The day proved clear, the atmosphere pure and exhilarating and our entire day's ride in and among the islands of the East Coast proved exceptionally enjoyable. Arrived at Bar Harbor at

teamer Lewiston *landing at Bar Harbor,*
irca 1879.

121

Bear Island Light, 1883, above. Saturday, August 4. *"... and finally Southwest Harbor. At several points I was forcibly reminded of similar views along the west coast of Scotland—the rock-bound islands with irregular bluffs exposed to the storms of centuries."*

Eagle Lake, Mt. Desert, 1883, right. Sunday, August 5. *Henry climbed to the summit of Green Mountain in exactly two hours and eight minutes and from there had a magnificent view of Eagle Lake.*

about 2 P.M. and were met at the wharf by Miss Dolly and Miss Emily Warder and their uncle, Mr. Price, who had kindly obtained rooms for us at the *Birch Tree Inn,* a quiet unpretentious hotel admirably located for the full enjoyment of all that was going on—comfortable cottage adjacent.

Sunday, August 5. Attended service at 9½ A.M. at Episcopal Chapel. During the afternoon ascended *Green Mountain,* on foot through the *gorge,* in company with Mr. DeWitt Knox of N.Y. Also strolled up Duck's brook and along "the rocks"—met Miss Bakewell and Miss Lea, etc. In fact the Island was filled with Philadelphians scattered more particularly among the three hotels, Lynan's Cottage, Rodick's and the Marlboro.

Bar Harbor from the Porcupines, 1883.
Tuesday, August 7. *Henry passed by the Porcupines after dark and may have missed ladies such as these taking measure of the drop.*

Eastport and Passamaquoddy Bay, circa 1839.

Tuesday, Aug. 7. Trip on *Frenchman's Bay* in the "Little Buttercup." Gloriously clear atmosphere and water quiet. Passed around *Iron Bound Island, Jordan, Stand, Calf, Simpson's, Bean's* and other islands. To *Sullivan*, for dinner at the Waukeag House. Music at the piano, and some dancing afterwards. Thence to *Handcock Point* and across to the *Ovens*, where we hailed George and Miss Horning and Miss Ellen who had driven up from Bar Harbor, but could not persuade them to come on board. Thence around and among the "Porcupines," and returned home—twenty-two in the party.

Wednesday, Aug. 8. Drove to *Jordon's Lake*, and enjoyed some boating in the morning, and to *Schooner Head* and *Otter Cliffs* during the afternoon. Buckboards used for all driving.

Thursday, Aug. 9. Drove across the island to Somesville, ordered dinner en route. Sauntered over to Beech Mt. with Miss Ellen and wandered through the ravine. Returned and dined at Somesville. After dinner rowed across *Somes harbor* with Miss Dolly Warden and Miss L. Lockwood and around *Bar Island* into *Somes Sound.* Carried boat across the bar, east side of island, and Miss Lockwood rowed home to Somesville.

Saturday, Aug. 11. Left about 2:30 P.M. by Steamer *Lewiston* for the north. When passing out of Frenchman's Bay into the ocean passed through immense beds of sea-weed which gave a reddish brown color to the water, an effect which the captain assured us was most unusual. Stopped at *Millbridge* and *Jonesport.* Large sardine

The landing at the Owen, Campobello, 1883. Sunday, August 12. *"After some little delay at the fishing village of* Lubeck, *took the little pilot sail-boat and crossed to the wharf of the* Owen at Campobello Island." *Writing of the hotels on* Campobello, Henry noted: *"These hotels give one a better idea of the accommodations offered to tourists in Switzerland or among the English Lakes of Cumberland than any others at summer resorts that I have thus far met in America."*

factories at both places. During the twilight, passed in close proximity to *gull rocks* the whole upper surface of which, for acres in extent, was covered with the white gulls, so thick as to make it appear snow covered as in winter. A blast from the steam whistle on board set the huge flock in motion, filling the air with frightened birds calling and fluttering wildly to get farther away. Entered the bay and harbor of *Machiasport* about 8 P.M. nearly colliding with a U.S. Revenue Cutter which lay at anchor almost in mid-channel. At Machiasport took a carriage and drove to the town of *Machias*, four miles, where we remained over night at the *West End.*

Sunday, Aug. 12. After a stroll through Machias, a neat, cleanly, busy little place in the lumber district, took an open carriage, and with one trunk only (the rest had been sent from Bar Harbor south to Portland to meet us on our return) we drove across the neck of land, 28 miles, which separates Machias from *Lubeck upon Passamaquoddy Bay*; a four hours ride. After some little delay at the fishing village of *Lubeck,* took the little pilot sail-boat and crossed to the wharf of the *Owen at Campobello Island.* All greatly pleased with the Owen at Campobello, the refined taste displayed in appointments and arrangements about the hotel being in marked contrast for the better with the accommodations at the best houses at Bar Harbor. After an excellent dinner, took a stroll over to the *Lyn-Y-coed,* found the same admirable appointments and refined arrangements for comfort and rest as at the *Owen.* An effort has evidently been made by the

Somes Sound near Somesville, Mt. Desert, 1883. Thursday, August 9. *"After dinner rowed across* Somes Harbor *with Miss Dolly Warden and Miss L. Lockwood and around* Bar Island *into* Somes Sound."

THE OWEN

BREAKFAST.

FRUIT.

Coffee.   Tea.   Breakfast Cocoa.   Chocolate.

Broiled Scrod.   Fried Codfish.
Halibut.   Finnan Haddie.
Broiled Mackerel.   Fresh Salmon.

Beefsteak.   Mutton Chop.
Lamb Chop.   Ham.
Veal Cutlets.   Breakfast Bacon.

Cucumbers.   Lettuce.   Tomatoes.

EGGS.

Fried.   Boiled.   Poached.   Omelette.   Scrambled.

Stewed, French Fried, Lyonaise and Baked Potatoes.

Hot Rolls.   Corn Bread.   Graham Bread.   Brown Bread.
Dry Toast.   Butter Toast.   Oatmeal.
Griddle Cakes.

Breakfast, 7 to 9.30.   Dinner, 1.30 to 3.   Supper, 6 to 8.

Breakfast menu, the Owen at Campobello Island, July 14, 1883.

DINNER.

Soup.
Lobster Chowder.
Mulligatawny.

Fish.
Baked Stuffed Cod, Tomato sauce.
Cucumbers.

Boiled.
Leg of Lamb, Caper sauce.
Corned Beef.
Chicken, Bachemel sauce.

Roast.
Spring Lamb, mint sauce.   Sirloin of Beef.
Stuffed Veal.   Turkey.

Entrees.
Calves Head and Brain sauce.
Chicken Croquettes aux Champignons.
Salmi of Venison with Olives.

Vegetables.
Mashed Potatoes.   Florida Potatoes.
Green Peas.   Lima Beans.   Sugar Corn.

Pastry
AND
Dessert.
Baked Rice.
Apple Pie.   Squash Pie.
Lemon Drops.   Assorted Cake.
Ginger Ice Cream.   Floating Island.
Fruits.   Nuts.   Raisins.
Coffee.   Cheese.

July 14th, 1883   T. A. BARKER, Manager.

Dinner menu, the Owen, July 14, 1883.

management to retain as much as possible the style of the "old country," and avoid the rough americanisms which thrust themselves forward at most of our watering places. The charming excursions from Campobello are equal to those of any other district in Maine for variety, and the "home comforts" far superior. For the quiet enjoyment of sailing, fishing and moderate driving, Campobello would seem to be the most desirable locality. Later in the afternoon our party drove to *Herring's Cove Beach.* Attended service at sundown in the Episcopal Church, some of the party hearing the English service for the first time.

Monday, Aug. 13. Joined a party arranged by Mr. Porter, the Roosevelt's, etc., on little steamer *Escort* for trip over to the *Island of Grand Manan.* Finally anchored in the Bay opposite *North Head village.* Lunch on board. Found Mrs. Cunningham (nee Lottie Wade) and family stopping at the little hotel on the Island. While the rest of the tourists were waiting for carriages, walked across the island, three miles, to *Long's Eddy* near *Money Cove,* and there all hands joined the *Escort* which had steamed around from North Head. In the mean time a smart breeze had come up, and fog commenced to collect along the bluffs. The sea became rougher, and Indians hurrying past us in their birch canoes, evidently to get into more sheltered localities from the coming storm, gave us a realizing sense of the uncertainty of the climate along this wild coast. We were obliged to board the *Escort* from the row boat, one party being dangerously near swamping from overloading the boat on the way out. Our departure was in marked contrast with our arrival. Almost everyone a little nervous, more or less, lest the blow should increase. After tossing about on the waves considerably, we finally passed through the fog, which continued to hug the Grand Manan coast, and getting the breeze on the port quarter instead of ahead made good time for the north end of *Campobello.* Once in the lee of the island we were again in quiet water. The sail up the bay was truly delightful, and finally the hotel comforts made a fitting finish to a glorious day. In the evening had some piano music in the parlor.

Tuesday, Aug. 14. Left the Owen at 10:15 A.M. after some little music in the parlor and prospects of a cordial good time if one had remained. Crossed by steamer to *Eastport,* and made close connection with the steamer up the St. Croix for *Calais.* Glorious ride up the *St. Croix River.* At *Calais,* took a carriage and drove around town, also through St. Stephens opposite, on the Canadian side of the river. Large cotton mills have recently been erected at St. Stephens. American capital—but being over the border certain duties, etc. are avoided.

Wednesday, Aug. 15. By rail to *McAdam Junction,* thence via *Bangor* to *Portland.* Found the *Prebble* a more desirable hotel than the Falmouth had been.

Lighthouse, Head Harbor, Campobello, 1883.

Thursday, Aug. 16. *Portland* to *Boston* via Eastern R.R. to the *Brunswick*. While walking during the evening noticed the extremely beautiful appearance of the foliage and parterres of flowers in the public garden now lit by electric lights—moonlight.

Friday, Aug. 17. By rail to *Dedham*, with Miss Horning. Saw the old Quincy Mansion, and "powder house" of revolutionary memory. Left Boston by afternoon train for Fall River, and thence by Steamer *Pilgrim* to *Newport*. Remained at Newport several days. Called on Mr. and Mrs. W. T. Richards (artist) at their cottage. Fishing off the reefs—cliff walk—driving on the Avenue, etc., tennis. Very many finer cottages erected in Queen Anne style since I was last at Newport. Visited the *Channing Memorial*.

Tuesday, Aug. 21. Left at 9 P.M. in Steamer *Old Colony* for *New York*. Went to Bob's in *Jersey City*.

Thursday, Aug. 24. Returned home and found George and Harry Pitcher, settled in the library at the *bachelor's roost*.

Mountains and Lakes

The steamer Jessie at Jerry's Landing, Conesus Lake, circa 1882. With flags flying, steam up, the Jessie stands ready for its scenic ride around the lake. The lake was Rochester's summer playground, and its shores were lined with summer cottages nestled among the trees.

The Catskills

Hudson River steamboats—"shoes with segars stuck on them"—brought visitors in 1827 to the Catskill Mountain House and soon it became the place to go, glittering with lights, the sound of pianos, and the hum of gaiety. The host was polite and gentlemanly; his table and rooms had all the luxuries of the city. In 1840 an English visitor wrote of the glorious bird's-eye view from her room—the Green Mountains of Vermont to the left and the Hudson and rich plains of Connecticut beyond.

George W. Curtis, gentleman-journalist, described the coach ride up the mountain in the rain:

"It was not cool inside the coach, but without, the wind was in high frolic with the rain . . . cold and very wet. Then the showers swept along a little, and we threw up the curtains and breathed fresh air, and about three miles from the Mountain House, where the steep ascent commences . . . I jumped out of the stage and walked. . . . The road climbs at first in easy zigzags and presently pushes straight on through the woods, and upon the side of a steep ravine. Two hours before sunset we stood upon the plateau before the Mountain House."

The Mountain House had for its feature "sunrising," or watching the sun come up from the bowl of night. Just before sunrise, employees of the hotel raced through the corridors with shouts loud enough to rouse the soundest sleepers. The guests, according to their wishes, could watch the sun from their warm chambers or stand shivering in the cool mountain air on the platform in front of the hotel.

Another specialty of the Mountain House was a trip of about two miles to the Kaaterskill Falls by carriage or on foot. The footpath was the shorter way, but woe to the guest who did not wear boots and keep an eye out for snakes! A refreshment stand, a pleasant cafe, stood at the very top of the falls and one might regenerate his spirits with a brandy

"Pic-nic party fishing," Hudson River, circa 1880. An English traveler wrote about the Hudson River: "I had generally heard the Hudson compared to the Rhine but my want of taste would no more admit of such a comparison than it would that New York and London should be mentioned in the same breath." Later, the journalist George Curtis replied that there was no littleness about the Hudson as there was about the Rhine. "The Danube has in part glimpses of such grandeur, the Elbe has something of such delicately penciled effects, but no European river is so lordly in its bearing—none flows in such state to the sea."

A young visitor to the Catskills, circa 1879.

The Catskill Mountain House, circa 1876. "There is an excellent hotel on an elevation of 2,212 feet above the level of the Hudson which gives an atmosphere of refreshing coolness amid the most sultry heat of summer." The brilliant white Mountain House, for more than three-quarters of a century, survived the ups and downs of a fickle tourist trade. During summer when the weather was good, the Mountain House overflowed with guests, and the surplus slept on the dining-room floor.

A view of the mountains, circa 1863, above.

Dancing Pavilion, Catskill Mountain House, circa 1875. At the Mountain House, guests could enjoy a dance and a spectacular view at the same time.

punch, a cooling ice cream, or a glass of sparkling lemonade. The cafe gentleman was also in charge of "letting the water" from a dam just above the falls. When a party of visitors arrived he would activate the falls to its full power. The water would gush violently over the top, appearing a small version of Niagara Falls.

A steep stairway could be used (for a quarter) to the foot of the falls. A guide waited at the base to take visitors on the narrow ledge behind the falls and onto a field of green grass on the opposite side, a delightfully cool spot for a picnic or refreshments. Visitors could now signal the alert cafe gentleman, standing on his piazza above, to send down by pole, rope, and baskets sundry bottles of the "coolest champagne ever tasted outside the vineyards of France." After resting on the mossy couch visitors could retrace their steps or follow the stream as it cascaded down the gorge for about a mile, then return to the Mountain House by road.

One of the pleasures of the Catskills before 1870 was the all-night camp. Groups of ten to twenty adventuresome people were formed, often more ladies than men, and several guides and a sturdy carriage were hired. After food, baggage, and bottles were loaded, the genial party went off to conquer High Peak, one of the highest points in the Catskill Mountains. The fun and merriment began when the road ended and the party took off on an overgrown footpath meandering through bush and forest, over and around rocks, some six miles into the wilds. The hike was enlivened with much yelling—did you see the bear, or the snake, or the panther? And there was the search for odd-looking personages playing at ninepins, or for the place where Rip Van Winkle had slept for twenty years.

View from the top of Kaaterskill Falls, looking down the Glen, circa 1867. From the time of Thomas Cole onward, artist-visitors came with sketchbooks to capture the beauties of the Catskills.

One of the best places to start doing the sights was at the famous Kaaterskill Falls. A refreshment café stood at the very top of the falls, where the genial gentleman who was in charge of turning on the water of the falls dispensed spirits and other refreshments. A steep wooden stairway descended to the bottom of the ravine.

View from the Guymard House, circa 1873. A Victorian "playground." In the evening the teetering seesaw was cleared away for the dance.

The ladies, sturdy and game, dressed in bloomer rigs, proved not to be the weaker sex. After counsel with the guides, the campsite chosen was usually under the ledge of Trysting Rock. (The mountains abounded with trysting rocks.) The party set to work felling trees, gathering hemlock sprigs for lean-tos and moss for bedding, building a small cooking fire and a big bonfire for the "sit around" when it got dark. High moon was thought to be the best time for storytelling, fun, and songs, and the party would gather up close as the cold of the mountains crept in from the ghostly forest. In the morning when the cookout breakfast was over the party, looking like straggly pioneers, retraced their way to the comforts of the hotel.

The Catskill Mountain House held undisputed sway as the king of resorts catering to sedate vacationers until the seventies. Nearby smaller boardinghouses, including Laurel House, took in the overflow. Then the explosion started, as in other resort areas, with new hotels, new railroads, and more steamers up the Hudson. The summertime Catskill was discovered—clean, fresh air "more pure than Switzerland," some said, and within weekend commuting distance of New York City. In 1871 the first of the big modern hotels, the Overlook Mountain House, opened its doors. It had probably the loftiest elevation of any hotel in the state and was modern in every way when compared to the often-renovated Catskill Mountain House. The Overlook had gas lighting, a fashionable mansard roof, and an electric telegraph. The dining hall had round and square tables with a waiter for each, whereas Mountain House visitors still ate at long board-inghouse-style tables.

Rumor had it that President Grant would come to stay at the Overlook, and in late summer of 1873 the star of many watering places finally arrived, in company as usual with his coterie of politicians. The hotel put on the customary band and choral shows, but the old gentleman was soon in his cups and had to be put to bed.

The Overlook Mountain House, near Rondout, 1871. The Overlook Mountain House opened its doors in the spring of 1871. The first up-to-date hotel with a capacity of five hundred, it had gas lighting, postal and telegraph service, printed menus, and a waiter for each table. It was said to have made many summer visitors happy during its short life; it burned to the ground on April 1, 1875.

Profile Lake, Franconia Notch, circa 1868, sometimes called "Old Man's Washbowl."

The White Mountains of New Hampshire

Off to the mountains—to breathe the pure, cool air, to wonder at the crystal-clear lakes, and to wade in the foaming water cascading down from mountain brooks. The seashore was not for everyone; thousands chose instead mountain greenery, freshwater lakes, and high places. Even foreign visitors were impressed with the beauty of the White Mountains of New Hampshire. Anthony Trollope, the English novelist and traveler, wrote:

"That there is a district in New England containing mountain-scenery superior to much that is yearly crowded by tourists in Europe, that it is to be reached with ease by railways and stagecoaches, and that it is dotted with huge hotels almost as thickly as they lie in Switzerland, I had no idea."

The routes to the White Mountains were numerous, even in the 1850s, and the roar of blasting powder was to be heard as pathways of travel opened up through deep forests and mountain slopes. The screech of locomotives barrelling along echoed in the quiet air. By the late 1870s nine first-class hotels charging five dollars a day handled from three to five hundred people each. A score of secondary hotels and hundreds of boardinghouses had accommodations for all tastes and pocketbooks, and a rustic farmhouse with do-it-yourself entertainment was only five dollars weekly.

A journal written by an old gentleman in 1854 told of railroad travel.

"Came by rail to Portland, in peril of life and limb. Stirred up with fifty plebeians treading on your toes and jostling your elbows. This modern improvement of cattle-pens over a gentleman's carriage with select and elect friends, and time to enjoy a beautiful country, is the 'advance of civilization?' Travelers now are prisoners under sentence of death."

Carriages in front of the Senter House, circa 1872. "The situation of the Hotel itself is unequaled for picturesque beauty in New England, while the charming drives in all directions, whether skirting the shores of the beautiful Lake or winding among the hills, introduce the traveller to the marvelous scenery of the surrounding country, sung by the poet Whittier, as 'The Heart of the Highlands.'"

Pemigewasset House, Plymouth, circa 1866. Trains bound for the White Mountains made the Pemigewasset House a mealtime stopover point. Passengers could enjoy a repast in the hotel's dining room or dine modestly in the café. Or a visitor could stay over in Plymouth to see the spot where Daniel Webster made his first speech or where Nathaniel Hawthorne breathed his last.

Kiarsarge House, North Conway, circa 1873. From an advertisement for the Kiarsarge: "The House is lighted with gas, contains Bath-rooms, Barber's-room, Billiard Hall, and all the modern improvements found in first-class hotels. The table will be supplied with all the luxuries of the season, and served in the best manner by experienced cooks."

The Senter House, Center Harbor, looking up from the shore of Lake Winnipesaukee, circa 1872. The editor of Harper's Monthly Magazine vacationed at the Senter House in August of 1862, and carped: "It is a good house at Center Harbor, with a pleasant old-fashioned flavor.... But there are two maple-trees upon the other side of the road in front which serve to cut off view of Ossipee [hill] and are of no other use ... the maple-trees are in the way."

The Great Dining Hall, Fabyans, 1888. The new Fabyan House was an easy place to get to—the railroad from Boston terminated in the front yard and the Portland line stopped a few miles away.

Abbot Square, Nashua, croquet party, circa 1871. Tourists going from New York to the White Mountains had to change trains at Nashua. If connections were poor, the town had three good hotels and croquet in the square.

Tip-Top House, Mount Washington, 1871.

At their destination the travelers were herded into a sturdy open-sided wagon used to take guests to hotels or on short excursions. Sometimes the wagons were fitted with rolled-up curtains at the sides that could be lowered when rainy.

Most visitors coming in by train to Gorham took one of these wagons or a coach out to the famous Glen House, an eight-mile uphill ride. Located not far from the base of Mount Washington, it was the most isolated of the large hotels, with a magnificent view of the Presidential Range to the front and to the rear the heavy ridges of Carter and Wildcat mountains. After a warm greeting from the landlord, visitors could expect a "capital" dinner.

A tourist guidebook wrote glowingly of the Glen House: "It would be difficult to conceive more complete arrangements for the accommodation of those who seek the mountain air or scenery. The romantic attraction of the locality—glens and gorges, streams, torrents, slides, lakelets, and waterfalls—are unequalled by those of any other mountain region."

For his first outing a visitor might choose a five-mile afternoon ride to Glen Ellis. By the time a guest had changed to riding clothes, a guide and horse would be waiting at the hotel door. Near Glen Ellis he would find a footpath descending to the foaming caldron. After an hour of leaping about from rock to rock he might retrace the path to his waiting horse and on the way back to the hotel admire the celebrated Crystal Cascade.

Another favorite side trip was following a brook to Thompson's Falls and down the well-trodden path leading to Emerald Pool, a lovely basin of water made famous in a painting by Albert Bierstadt. "At first one sees only a deep hollow, with a glassy pool at the bottom, and a cool light coming down through the high tree-tops. Large rocks are picturesquely posed about the margin. Upon one side a birch leans out over the pool, which reflects brilliantly from the polished surface the white light of the satin bark . . . black marble inlaid with arabesques of color."

The greatest attraction of the Glen House was its closeness to Mount Washington. Everyone liked to tell their friends back home that they had made the 6,293-foot ascent to the summit. The proprietor of the Glen House kept trained horses and experienced guides on hand for the trip. Ladies were told, "If a lady is in feeble health, or if very nervous temperament, she will find herself more comfortable to remain in the rocking chair. But if a lady is in ordinary health, and has the least love of adventure . . . let her by no means forego the pleasure of the enterprise." The hotel usually made up mixed parties of about fifteen to twenty, who set out at six in the morning for the day's outing. The party could rest a while at the summit and have a leisurely dinner at the Tip-Top House before the return trip.

By 1861 a good carriage road led from the Glen House to the summit, making it possible for visitors to travel by wagon. The ten-mile

Engine, Mount Washington Railroad, circa 1869. "Here the 'iron horse' guided by the hand of genius, climbs triumphantly to the dizzy height of 6,285 feet . . . where the 'storm king' riding on the wings of the whirlwind, has hitherto reigned supreme!" Later, engines would have a cab to protect the engineer from the elements.

Top to bottom:

Railroad to Mount Washington, at base, circa 1872. In the early days of the cog railway, coaches and carriages brought hotel guests from miles around to take the thrilling ride up the incline. It was said that "to stand upon the summit of Mount Washington is the culminating desire of every visitor to the mountain region. Here, from the highest point on the Atlantic slope, he can look down upon this vast panorama of hills and valleys, cities, and plains, dotted with a thousand silvery lakes blended into one harmonious whole."

Jacob's Ladder, Mount Washington, circa 1875. The locomotive had to puff a little harder when it reached the steepest part of the ascent, named after the biblical Jacob.

Inside the Tip-Top House, Mount Washington, August 17, 1871.

Echo Lake, Franconia Notch, circa 1869. "The fair bosom of Echo Lake, that brightest gem of the mountains, whose waters are of the most exquisite purity and clearness, and are furrowed throughout the summer of a flotilla of pretty pleasure-boats."

The Waltz, circa 1850. Dances or "hops" were held several times a week at resort hotels. Getting up a hop was quite simple—a subscription paper was sent down the table at dinner, and if enough patrons subscribed to meet expenses, word went out quickly and guests at other hotels were invited. Although the waltz was condemned by some as being an utter abomination for a lady of delicacy and refinement, it remained popular throughout the century.

road was steep and in places quite narrow. One old-time driver said, "There should be no fooling, no chaffing, and no drinking on that road." Travelers told of feeling suspended in midair during the swift descent.

Mount Washington became so popular with summer people that a local engineer, Sylvester Marsh, decided to build a cog railroad to the top. Mr. Marsh took quite a ribbing about his "ride to the moon." Though only three miles to the summit, the grade had a rise of one foot in three, but by 1869 the railway was completed, with safety features that satisfied even the timid. The fare of six dollars was not too much for such a thrilling ride that lasted for an hour and a half.

One of the most beautiful regions in the White Mountains was westward in the Franconia Mountain Range. A tourist attraction, the Old Man of the Mountain, "the cold, sharp human profile chiseled in colossal proportions by the hand of nature," was passed before reaching the hotel. Soon the large, rambling Profile House came in view, standing just beyond shimmering Echo Lake in a setting of rich green forest. Echo Lake and a freak of nature, the Flume, were the greatest attractions of the area. "As we wander down from the Profile House to the little pebbly beach that borders the lake . . . we see reflected all the giant forms around us. While we sit here enjoying its quiet beauty, and watching the flight of eagles in the air, perhaps we hear the note of a bugle from the little boat that takes passengers to the middle of the lake. . . ." From the lake back to the Profile House the path led by Eagle Cliff, where eagles built their nests.

The absence of pollen was one of the important reasons so many people favored the White Mountains during the summer. The clergyman Henry Ward Beecher summered in the mountains, to escape hay fever, and preached every Sunday under a tent. Another allergic, a young lady of good family but empty purse, shocked her parents by becoming a summer waitress at one of the large hotels. She went to the hotel in disguise and later wrote of her experiences for Godey's Lady's Book. Her salary was four dollars a week, with one evening off, and she slept in a garret with the other female help.

140

The Fabyan House, White Mountains, 1879. The new Fabyan House was an easy place to get to—the railroad from Boston terminated in the front yard, and the one from Portland stopped but a few miles away. Before Horace Fabyan built his new hotel, he often entertained his guests by firing a cannon or blowing a bugle, so they could listen to the echo. "In reply to the call, seven separate echoes are audible, each one distinct and varying . . . . No adequate idea of this peculiar melody can be conveyed by mere words . . . and, once heard can never be forgotten."

Excursion at Webster Lake, Franklin, circa 1869.

The Flume, near Franconia Notch, circa 1871. The Franconia region had two great natural wonders – the giant profile of the Old Man of the Mountain and an 800-foot chasm called The Flume. The only time visitors could tour the attraction was during the dry season. Just above the walkway at the Flume's entrance was an immense rounded block of granite, apparently supported by thin air, which seemed poised and ready to fall on the visitor.

Many summer sojourners stayed at one of the several picturesque mountain villages, perhaps staying at an old farmhouse with nooks and crannies and a big broad porch shaded with old elms and maples, or in houses near sparkling lakes. Lazy days were spent exploring and climbing mountains or going on sketching tours. Sketchbooks recorded pretty scenery that would be embellished during the winter months. Many young women liked to gather and press ferns or wild flowers. Some brought along books to read on a quiet hillside; others preferred driving about the countryside. Amateur botanists roamed the mountain ridges in search of plants not found elsewhere in New England. And if there was not enough activity there was always lawn croquet.

Saratoga Springs

Where did one send daughters to find a rich husband? Where did beautiful ladies show off the latest Paris fashions and fabulous jewels? Where did intellectual, stylish, fast men find an atmosphere sparkling with wit and innuendo? Saratoga Springs, of course—the queen of American watering places and Cupid's summer home.

Saratoga Springs became a fashionable watering place in 1803 when Gideon Putnam opened the big, rambling Union Hotel. By 1828 four good-sized hotels had been built and fifteen hundred people a week were coming into town during the season. One of the resort's annual visitors was former Emperor Joseph Bonaparte. He found at the plush old United States Hotel the luxuries of public reading rooms, a library, ballrooms, and a hotel newspaper. In the early days cards were seldom seen, but backgammon and checkers were played in the barrooms. One English visitor in 1828 thought it disgraceful that everyone rode everywhere—in gigs, dearborns, or open carriages—quite different from the English habit of walking.

Another foreign tourist wrote in 1833 about all kinds of people—some with money, others with little, young aspirants, matrons, and irresponsible old gentlemen. Accommodations were splendid, he said, with spacious piazzas and dining rooms, though the bedchambers were ill-furnished and inconvenient. The daily routine began about ten o'clock, when many guests would leave by rail for Ballston Springs, Schenectady, or Albany. Billiards, reading, and visiting were popular morning pursuits. Dinner was served at 3:00 P.M.—what a rush when the dinner bell rang! After dinner, introductions were made all around to the ladies in the drawing room—then off for a pleasant drive in the country. In the evening, tea and supper were followed by balls, cotillion parties, and an occasional concert by wandering minstrels.

Congress Hall for years reigned as the fashionable spot in Saratoga. Nathaniel Willis wrote in 1840 that guests were like packed herrings. "A guest's bed, chair, and wash-stand, resemble those articles as seen

Lawn view of the new United States Hotel, circa 1874.

Two gentlemen in Congress Park, opposite. Here was a place for quiet contemplation, for higher thoughts – of music and art. A very different world from the veranda of the Congress Hall Hotel, the inner sanctum where portly equals met each morning, bowed, lit their cigars, and engaged in conversations on money and politics.

An afternoon in Congress Park, circa 1885.

Congress Hall Hotel and Park, 1902. "No park of equal size in the United States can be compared with it for beauty of natural scenery or elegance of architecture and artistic ornaments."

Broadway, United States Hotel. Strolling down the tree-lined avenue in Saratoga, one might encounter many elegantly dressed vacationers. Carriages for hire lined up in front of the swank hotels to catch monied patrons. In season the cost for a party of four to drive to the lake and back, in a fancy turnout with a coachman dressed like a drum major, was $6. The thrifty tourist could make it for half the amount in a common rig. And, of course, there was always the more accessible pleasure of enjoying the day in town.

Congress Park Pagoda and Lake, 1870. For those tired of the water cure, there were always the pleasures of the lake and parks. Fun in Saratoga was a far cry from busy Coney Island. Daytime amusement in the queen of the resorts was a shady walk, a cozy ride around the lake, or, perhaps, a row in a hired boat.

Dining Hall, Grand Union Hotel, 1882. Saratoga was an indoor town when it came to gala social events. During the 1860s the hotel entertained many celebrities, and in the 1870s Grant held several receptions here during his term as President. In a town where everything was colossal, the Grand Union boasted of the "Largest Dining Hall in the World."

in penitentiaries; and if he chanced to be ill at night, he might die like a Pagan, 'without bell or candle.' " Hotel residents were wakened by a bell at 7:30 A.M. and another at 8:00 A.M., punctuality being of utmost importance for a hot breakfast. The dinner hour had moved up to 2:00 P.M., and the afternoon drive had to be brief, because tea—a meal consisting of cold meats, hot rolls, cakes, berries, pies, and other delicacies—was served at six. When the evening festivities began, the large colonnade became thronged with people. If the evening was ball night, guests were alerted that the dance had begun when "Hail, Columbia" was struck up by the black band. The ballroom (the dining room by day) was lit with a suspended hoop bound with evergreens and stuck around with candles. The couples arrived arm in arm, stealing away during the dancing for a breath of fresh air on the colonnade. At eleven o'clock champagne was served to the ladies and the gentlemen retired to the bar, after which "the candle burns brighter, and everybody is much more agreeable."

In 1844 Willis wrote about the United States Hotel, advising young girls—"Take your papa there 'for his health,' my dear belle! And tell him, too, that it was the well-expressed opinion of the philosopher Bacon that 'money, like manure, is offensive if not spread.' Tell your mamma to tell him how pale he is when he wakes in the morning! Tell the doctor to prescribe Congress water without the taste of the cork! Tell him, if he does not, and you are not let go with a chaperon, you will do something you shudder to think of—bolt, slope, elope . . ." Addressing their parents, he wrote in 1844: "The primitive confidingness of American girlhood . . . has been abandoned for the European mammadom and watchful restraint. . . . What it seeks to

Out for a drive, circa 1890. "The American gentleman is as good a type of his class as is to be found in London or Paris, but he has less stiffness of manner . . . he is probably not as well educated as the average English gentleman, for, in the first place, no leisure-class exists, and the position of an idler is hardly recognized . . . they have at least more general intelligence—they 'use their intellects.' "

Grand Union Hotel, circa 1875.

supplant or remedy, and among other evils is that of making culpable what was once thought innocent. I do not believe we shall grow purer by Europeanizing."

Willis wrote that the coming season would be one with the crowded "uncomfortableness of splendour." True to his prediction, a letter from a friend confirmed a "most undesirable uncomfortableness," offering other complaints too. "There used to be dandies. That was in the time when there was an aristocracy in the country. With the leveling (from the middle to the top), that has been going on for the last ten or twelve years, the incentive, somehow, seems gone . . . there are no dandies! Only one dandy at Saratoga—among three thousand fashionables!" Belles at Saratoga, he said, were "well-born, well-moulded and well-dressed." Of these, five or six were beautiful, fifty or sixty endowed with

Portrait of Saratoga belles, circa 1872. "Rise and dress; go down to the spring; drink to the music of the band; walk around the park—bow to gentlemen; chat a little . . . see who comes in on the train; take a siesta; walk in the parlor; bow to gentlemen; have a small talk with gentlemen; have some gossip with ladies."

A hop in the new ballroom of the Grand Union, 1876. "The three largest hotels have elegant ball-rooms, where hops take place every evening. Balls are held every week at each of the houses. Upon the latter occasion, the dressing becomes a matter of life and death, and explains why such numbers of those traveling arks known as Saratoga trunks are docked at the station every summer."

beauty enough to make a dull man happy. Moreover, some were wearing "a kind of short gown, never before seen but at the wash tub, but promoted for the drawing-room! Fancy a buttoned up frock-coat over a snowy petticoat—to breakfast." (The dress had been dug up by the spirited belles of Carolina and was called a jib-along-josey.)

Another observer told of old women popping out of their rooms to call a waiter with their wigs off, lazy men coming to breakfast unshaved, and bustles flattened out by dinner chairs into upright pianos. When a gentleman had dressed in the morning, he had only to sit on a sofa for ten minutes and every known female of his hotel acquaintance was ready to talk—a far cry from the hard-to-get New York City belles. Some men were wearing "these gathered French trousers—making a man into a 'big-hipped bumble bee'—as if we needed to be more like women! I see, too, that, here and there a youth has a coat padded over the hips!"

The daily routine continued much the same in the early 1850s. A popular journalist of the day wrote in 1852:

151

Some of the lovely ladies of the era, pictured in Godey's *magazine, 1865.*

"We discuss the new arrivals. We criticise dresses, and styles, and manners. We discriminate the Arctic and Antarctic Bostonians, fair, still, and stately, with a vein of scorn in their Saratoga enjoyment, and the languid, cordial, and careless Southerners, far from precise in dress or style, but balmy in manner as a bland southern morning. We mark the crisp courtesy of the New Yorker, elegant in dress, exclusive in association, a pallid ghost of Paris—without its easy elegance. . . . We discover that exclusiveness is not elegance. But while we laugh at Saratoga, its dancing, dressing, and flirtation . . . it is an oasis of repose in the desert of our American hurry. . . ."

Criticism was a favorite pastime. It was reported that the hotel was making a fortune from invalids.

"The innkeepers . . . have 'ducked to the gilded mob'; and grown heavy with gains, have pushed our poor amusement-seekers to the worst shifts of crowded tables, and of attic chambers."

Another wrote: "Those horrid waiters will tramp in like an army, and crush any conversation I may attempt, and ruin my dinner with their abominable flourishes of pewter dishcovers. After dinner I light up a cigar and listen to 'that eternal band.' " He further gossiped that after dancing on a hot night the girls went to their rooms at 1:00 or 2:00 A.M., but the men took cobblers and cigars at the bar and retired about 3:00 A.M. At nine or ten in the morning, guests appeared in extraordinary costumes, and after eating an egg, a chop, and some kidneys made up parties to drive or play billiards.

An editor of a popular monthly magazine had his say in 1858. "A caravanserai crowded with rich people, and drinkers, and dancers; belles bowling in muslin and flirting in a public parlor; very young men gambling and getting drunk, and sick with tobacco; an army of black waiters manoevering in the dining-hall; people polking themselves into perspirations; a scraggy green square patch with starved Germans tooting on wind-instruments after dinner; and people full of ditto languidly toddling round."

Something new came to Saratoga in the mid-sixties. A racecourse was laid out about a mile from Congress Spring. Harness racing had been popular in the 1850s, but now the most famous racehorses in the country were brought in for events in the middle of July and in the second week of August. During the excitement, every hotel, boardinghouse, and private house was crowded to overflowing. Innkeepers housed visitors in every nook and cranny.

Lady leaders of fashion by the end of August finally exhausted the gorgeous contents of enormous trunks—often as many as twenty-five of them brought for the season. Society columnists reported it all: "Miss Brown, of ———, a charming graceful blonde, was attired in a rich white corded silk, long train, with ruffles of the same, overdress of pink grosgrain . . . with satin bows and point lace, hair à la Pompadour,

Saratoga Morrisey's Gambling House, 1871.

Saratoga Race-Course, 1875. The best of America's thoroughbreds raced at Saratoga in the middle of July and the second week of August. The town's hotel owners and innkeepers had to use all their ingenuity to care for the huge sporting crowd. When the racecourse was laid out in 1866, it was considered unsurpassed except by the famous "Fashion" track on Long Island.

Congress Spring. "Multitudes flock here during the summer months, but their stay is usually limited to a few brief weeks—a time, in many cases, too short for these mild, natural remedies to accomplish their perfect work. Thousands of visitors, therefore, find it necessary to continue the use of waters after leaving the springs." Some visitors stayed in water-cure boardinghouses such as Dr. Strong's, on Circular Street, where the residents could enjoy prayers and sermons daily. Here doctors used various forms of hydrotherapy; a "vacuum cure" and "movement cure" were featured, as were superb facilities for Turkish or Russian baths. Dr. Strong's remained open year-round and was said to in no way give the appearance of being a place for invalids.

with curls on white feathers, pearls and diamonds. . . . Miss Brown is the accomplished daughter of Mr. Brown, one of the leading citizens of the metropolis."

In the evening Saratoga took on a festive air; faces were alight with reflections from gas lamps and candles. Hotel parlors were filled with beautifully dressed ladies and the wide piazzas with gentlemen eager for cigars and conversation. Even the lighted streets were crowded with strollers in fashionable attire. The hotel ballrooms glowed with expensive chandeliers sparkling like diamonds. An admission of one dollar was customary at the balls, and elegant refreshments were served. On ball nights the grounds of the Grand Union Hotel were illuminated by colored Chinese lanterns which, combined with the brilliant gas jets of the ballroom, made a pretty and romantic setting.

Once horse racing had become established at Saratoga, another vice soon crept in, a gambling club. John Morrissey, the politician of bare-knuckle prize-fighting fame, built a gambling house in 1870. Journals all over the country carried accounts about the gorgeous furnishings, soft carpets, and faro parlors. During the first summer, twenty-five thousand ladies visited the rooms and several receptions were held. Although Morrissey was well liked by many of the locals because of his financial aid, the Young Men's Christian Association brought suit against the club in an attempt to close its doors. After the club changed hands in 1894, its name was changed to the Casino and it was refurbished in an ostentatious manner. It was said that fabulous sums of money were won and lost at the establishment.

In the 1880s shocking reports continued, this time about the "fashionable immodesty" at the United States Hotel, and modes of makeup and dress. In August 1881 a reporter wrote of dyed hair, plucked eyebrows, and dark lines drawn below the eye to "throw out the pupil." Many ladies wore gray wigs and made up their faces, coloring the lips and cheeks. The reporter saw one man with makeup and long, crimped hair that floated over his shoulders. He wore a handsome black dress suit and had a bow of silk crepe de chine at his "snowy" throat.

The scene continued much the same into the nineties, with brilliant balls at the grand hotels, music from top-name bands. It was a scene probably unsurpassed for fashion in the world: "It is Paris, London, and New York mingling in one glorious outing; it is Atlantic City with a greater dash of elegance, a more exalted tone. Gathered here for a few short weeks each year are the wealth, wit, beauty and fashion of the most eminent society . . . gay belles of the season, matrons proud of their social victories, and gilded youths from sparkling coteries. Less exclusive than Newport, society here embraces all that shines with an honorable and untarnished lustre."

The Green Mountains of Vermont

"Vermont, the Green Mountain State, may vie with any other section of the Union in picturesque beauties, mountain scenery, or invigorating climate. When we combine the mountain, lake, and river scenery of this State, together with her lovely valleys, she stands perhaps unrivalled as a resort for the tourist seeking health and pleasure."

The state of Vermont, sitting between the rugged White Mountains to the east and the Adirondack wilderness to the west, seemed a serene valley to the tourist, with its modest mountain peaks seldom higher than four thousand feet. Lake Champlain, separating Vermont from New York State, was a scenic attraction, and its well-built steamers provided luxurious, easy transportation to many points of interest. The steamers, coupled with an excellent network of railroads running through the state, gave easy access to mountains, springs, and lakes. Yet Vermont kept its quaint atmosphere of pleasant rural farms, neat little villages, and unspoiled scenery.

Tourists coming from Boston were advised not to miss the view of the Connecticut River forming the Vermont-New Hampshire border. The best spot for viewing was from the bridge where the river narrowed and flowed "with a power and rapidity that whitened its waters like a tide of snow flakes."

If the tourist was not in a hurry to reach Burlington, he could make a stopover at Rutland to see the famous Clarendon Springs. This summer resort catered to hundreds of people, many coming from great distances. Clarendon House advertised itself in 1876 as "a place for the businessman to recruit, and for families to spend the summer months . . . nothing here unpleasant—pure air, beautiful scenery, pleasant drives and walks, and above all, a spring of water which has no superior. It has no sediment, is delicious to drink, health giving, and, in bathing acts like a charm on the skin." Springwater was put up in

Hunter, Saxtons River, circa 1877.

The babbling brook, circa 1875.

High Bridge, Winooski, from below, circa 1869. A Green Mountain vacation was slow and gentle. It was an artist's scene in soft colors—low rolling hills set in green, weather-beaten covered bridges, and serene brooks and ponds. Sometimes a vacation party camped out on the shore of a lake or a bay where fishing, boating, and just loafing could be enjoyed for a modest outlay of money.

Congress Hall, Sheldon Springs, circa 1871.

The Bristol House, Bristol, circa 1875. Mr. O. K. Bucklin ran the only hotel in Bristol. A visitor could look the town over (which did not take long), go to Bartlett's Dam, climb Hogback Mountain, or go digging in the Indian burial grounds at Bristol Pond.

Fourth of July parade, circa 1890. On special days it was Vermont for the Vermonters, and the summer visitor had better stand back. The natives had their own way of doing things when it came to parades, homespun town fairs, and annual cemetery outings.

barrels and shipped to invalids who needed the water treatment after they left the hotel.

Clarendon Springs began early. In 1776 Asa Smith, a gentleman in poor health, had a dream about a spring that would restore him to health. He set off on a search. "Arriving at the spot, he recognized it as the one he had seen in his dream, and accordingly at once drank the water, and bound clay saturated with it on his swollen and inflamed limbs." Word spread of the man's cure, and people started coming in from all over the country. In the 1850s the place hummed with Southerners up for the cure.

When the traveler reached Burlington, on Lake Champlain, he was in the "queen city" of Vermont. The lake, at this point about ten miles wide, and the offshore islands and headlands, with a backdrop of distant mountains on both sides, made a fetching panorama. At Burlington the tourist had to make a decision—whether to take a steamboat south to Ticonderoga and Whitehall, or northward to Rouses Point and Montreal, Alternately, he might forego the steamer altogether and make a trip to Mount Mansfield, the highest mountain in Vermont, or to Camels Hump, another lofty peak, equidistant to the

Mount Mansfield, view of summit, with Philadelphia party, 1868. This is where the Philadelphia group gave up the rugged climb. The next year they went to Mount Washington, in the White Mountains, where they could go to the top by cog railroad.

View of Saint Johnsbury, circa 1873. The tiny rural towns of the Green Mountains offered the summer vacationer a way of life not found in any other resort areas.

Summit House, Mount Mansfield, Stowe, circa 1868. The easy way to climb Mount Mansfield was by the carriage road to the Summit House. The climb up the west side requiring the help of a cable was about as rough as any ordinary tourist might want. The visitors who came in June were wise to bring their "woolies" along.

southeast, both places reported in the travel guidebooks as romantic resorts.

If the visitor decided on Mount Mansfield, he boarded a train at Burlington and proceeded to Waterbury and Stowe, a little town at the foot of the mountains, by stage. A large resort hotel was built in Stowe in 1864 offering bowling and a pond for fishing and bathing, along with the thrills of mountain climbing. A carriage road ran from the village to the summit. The area near the top was heavily wooded where the road passed over a terrace of solid rock followed by a shaky corduroy bridge that spanned a chasm in the mountainside.

As the forest thinned, the visitor caught his first glimpse of the Summit House standing at the foot of a huge cliff known as the Nose. The Summit House not only had magnificent views from its veranda but also a feature for guests reminiscent of the Mountain House in the Catskills. Every morning when the sun was due to appear a bell was rung and a man shouted "Sunrise." A troop of sleepy guests staggered out to the balcony for the viewing.

160

Fishing idyll, circa 1872.

On the western side of Mount Mansfield a footpath led up to the Nose. It was a rugged climb, but tourists could manage with the help of a cable and were rewarded by one of the finest views in the country. After making the climb Emerson called Champlain the Lake of the Clouds. The blue waters of the lake and the ridges of the Adirondacks could be seen to the west, the distant White Mountains to the east, the popular Camels Hump and Killington Peak and the countless lower peaks of the Green Mountains to the south, and to the north, Jay Peak and Owls Head, the St. Lawrence River, Lake Memphremagog, and the spires of Montreal.

One of the special attractions of the Mount Mansfield area was Smugglers Notch, where once smugglers had hidden goods brought over from the Canadian border. The sides of the Notch rise to about a thousand feet. At the bottom of the ravine lay huge boulders and rocks covered with mosses and ferns, an artist's study in greens. The Notch was a sight to behold after a heavy rain, when the stream became a torrent and water cascaded over the cliffs in beautiful, misty patterns.

For mineral spring fanciers there was a choice of several delightful springs. Saint Albans was one, Weldon Springs another, its special water components being crenate of iron and iodide of magnesium. The water at neighboring Sheldon Springs was highly alkaline, pleasant to the taste, and reported to arrest cancer—many such cases were attested. Highgate Springs, beautifully situated on Missisquoi Bay, had a group of medicinal springs, fine boating and bathing, and good duck hunting and fishing. To the north was Newport, also known as the border city, a popular gateway between Canada and New England.

New York Lake Country

"We once again breathe the air, heavy with the odor of pines and cedar, or fragrant with the breath of blossoming clover. Again we wander among the daisies and buttercups that gem the hillside, sloping so gently down to where the wavelets kiss the white beach, or floating among the verdant islands watch the sunlight and shadows chase each other up the mountain side, while every crag and fleecy cloud is mirrored in the quiet water below."

North from Fort William Henry Hotel, Lake George, circa 1871. "Prices at the Fort William Henry Hotel are equal to any in the land." At $5 a day only the affluent could afford a vacation there. However, on occasion, an "aristocratic and high-toned" young clerk might slip in, dressed in faultless kids and paper cuffs, who would probably spend his year's savings for two weeks at a first-class hotel.

Lake George, on the verge of wilderness, had become by the 1840s a part of the fashionable tour, and the deer and eagle of earlier days were becoming scarce. Caldwell was a flourishing town built at the southern end of the lake, with a hotel well known for fancy sportsmen and scenery hunters.

Passengers got off the train at Glens Falls and made the rest of the journey to Caldwell by stage. In the 1870s this stage line, one of the finest in the country, used Concord coaches carrying up to thirty passengers. The nine-mile trip took an hour and a quarter. Only tried and trusted drivers were employed, their importance being likened to a "country undertaker conducting a first-class funeral." Travelers riding on the stage were often an odd kettle of fish. An Englishman might be aboard with notebook in hand—young ladies, happy to be there— mothers with precocious offspring—young college lads—all were represented.

As the stage slowed down at the foot of the hill outside Glens Falls, four ragged little fellows would dash out of the bushes and throw bunches of fragrant white pond lilies at the coach. Then they would hold out rimless tattered hats and beg for handouts. Collecting their plunder, they would settle down to wait for the next stage. It was said the boys made over six hundred dollars a season.

After a while George Brown's Half-way House was reached, where the passengers had five minutes for refreshments while the horses were

Colonnade of Fort William Henry Hotel, Lake George, circa 1872. Each evening until 11 o'clock, a celebrated band played in the 42-by-87-foot parlor, fronting on the lake. One romantic wrote: "Intoxicating music rose and fell on perfumed air, and the reeling senses floated in breathless ecstasy, as heart beating against heart, added fire to love's young flame."

Camping scene, Lake George, circa 1873. For some, camping out around Lake George meant a life of easy companionship, with few worries except deciding who would cook the next meal. For more orthodox campers, gray uniforms and white military caps were de rigueur, as were the proper camping and fishing procedures.

Tips from The Tourist's Guide *of 1871: "To prevent mosquitoes or gnats from annoying you—mix sweet oil and tar in equal parts . . . pour a little in your hand and annoint your face with it . . . . To reconcile the ladies to it, we add the fact that it renders the skin soft and smooth as an infant's."*

watered. Lemonade, milk punch, and soda pop on ice were for sale; also something a little stronger, lemonade with a "stick" (liquor) in it. Inside the Half-way House, passengers could look at a cabinet filled with old Indian curiosities and other relics picked up nearby on the old battlegrounds of the French and Indian War. Other features of Brown's were birds in cages, a flower-crowded porch, and at least thirty cats.

After leaving Brown's the ride was a changing panorama of scenic views and local historical sites of the French and Indian War, Bloody Pond, and Williams Monument. Colonel Ephraim Williams, commander of a regiment of Massachusetts troops, was ambushed and killed there in 1755.

On arriving at Caldwell, many travelers headed for the famous Fort William Henry Hotel. It had been enlarged in 1868 and was hardly recognizable from earlier days. It was now four to six stories high with a mansard roof and a long expanse of lake frontage. Inside the general office were "stage companies, telegraph office and cigar and book stand supplied with all the latest books, periodicals, daily papers and photographs." The drawing room was on one side; on the other were "suites of rooms, bijou parlors and the large billiard hall, while at the back is the grand dining room . . . from which guests can look out through the large doors across the shimmering waters to the blue mountains beyond." In all, it took two hundred people to run the hotel, including seventy-five waiters, eleven hall boys, seven porters, seven cooks, and innumerable lady dishwashers.

After the excitement of Saratoga, Lake George was like the morning after a ball—tranquil. "There is nothing to do but drive, sit on the hotel piazza, or go fishing on the lake." A journalist wrote in 1851 that "it is a good place to study fancy fishermen, who have taken their piscatory degrees on Wall and Pearl Streets."

Ultrarespectable visitors to Lake George stayed at a resort called Crosbyside, catering to about two hundred guests. Just across the lake from Caldwell, it could be reached by steamer or a short carriage ride through the woods and across the beach. Among the hotel's highly regarded guests were "Supreme Court judges, D.D.s, Japanese princes and escaped editors." One writer in 1873 said the guests "would be rather strong society for the average touring mortal if the balance of power was not retained . . . by the bevy of . . . young ladies who are annually banished from city homes by confiding mothers, satisfied that they will be safe with Mrs. Crosby (who seems especially designed by nature to bring up girls in the proper way)."

Most of the short-term visitors to Lake George stayed in hotels and boardinghouses in and around Caldwell. The lake was always busy with pleasure party boats, fishing, rowing, or exploring the many tiny islands in the thirty-four-mile area. The bright-colored costumes of the boaters, the sparkling pure water, and the background of blue skies and green mountains formed a scene to please an artist.

First-time visitors to Lake George always went over to stroll around the ruins of the old fort just east of the Fort William Henry Hotel. Afterward they sometimes walked north along the lakeshore to Healing Spring. The owner of the spring, Uncle Joe, told everyone who would listen (and many did) about the wonderful cures wrought by the springwaters.

If the vacationer chose to ride instead of walk, a trip up Prospect Mountain could be fun. A wagon was provided, a dollar pressed into the driver's hand sealed the bargain, and a lively ride began, often not without mishaps. Wheels reportedly fell off the wagon with alarming regularity.

Trips by boat to explore the many islands helped to while away many hours happily. Regular commercial steamboats plied back and forth on the lake, stopping at all places of interest. Private boats could also be hired with guide for from one to two dollars a day and from six to ten dollars a week. For larger pleasure parties, the steamboat *Owl* could be chartered for five dollars an hour or twenty-five dollars a day. Legend had it that treasure had been buried at Tea Island, a mile downlake from Caldwell, and the island had been dug over many times.

Next came some favorite camping places such as Sheldon's Point, visited every year by a party of graduates from C.C.N.Y., said by local people to be rising lights in the literary and professional worlds. They named their retreat Camp Manhattan, Manhattan being an Indian word meaning "a place where men get drunk." On the east side of the point was a small, homelike guest hotel, and under the mountain on the east shore was Trout Pavilion, a small hotel where Fourth of July dances were held. Just a little north of the pavilion, on Kattskill Bay, was the Kattskill House with its fine bathing beach. The mountains to the rear of the hotel made for good hunting, and fishing in the bay was always good.

Rowing on Kattskill Bay in front of the Kattskill House.

Camp life at Lake George.

Summer portrait, circa 1884.

Bolton, second in size to Caldwell and ten miles away, was connected to the neighboring town by three daily steamers and a delightful lakeside road. Permanent summer guests stayed here; there were few transients. The resort had several fine hotels, two of which were fairly large, catering to a class of guests who were a kind of cross between the dandies at the Fort William Henry and the hardy sportsmen found farther down the lake.

Nearby was Fourteen-Mile Island, a paradise for the serious sportsman. Fishing grounds around the island were tops, and accommodations reasonable. Farmhouses in the area charged about eight to nine dollars a week, compared to five dollars a day at the Fort William Henry Hotel.

At mid-century the great tourists' excursion was the round trip to Lake Champlain. One crossed Lake George on the morning boat, went overland by Baldwin's line of stages, had dinner at the Fort Ticonderoga Hotel with a stroll among the ruins, then took an afternoon ride on one of the elegant Champlain steamers, then back to Glens Falls by rail, returning to Caldwell by the regular stage arriving at 10:00 P.M.

For hardy folks who decided to penetrate deep into the Adirondack wilderness, Lake George tourists could take the morning stage to Pottersville, a twenty-four-mile trip. Civilization disappeared quickly as the road threaded through dense forests of oak and pine, by mountains, lakes, and ravines. From Pottersville travel schedules were touch and go for the 1870 visitor—coaches ran only twice a week to Minerva, and from there an open wagon ran just once a week to Long Lake. From Long Lake, where good accommodations were to be found, it was still another ten miles to popular Raquette, the largest of the interior lakes, where a sizable guest house had been built. At this point in the tour visitors could bridge the ponds, lakes, and streams by carrying the light boats from one body of water to the next.

B. F. De Costa, a historian of the Adirondack area, wrote in 1869: "The fishermen and the hunters are indeed in their element. For one, the lakes and streams are stocked with splendid fish, while for the other, the woods abound with every variety of game, from the wild-cat up to the deer, the moose, the wolf, the panther, and the bear. And as with beasts, so with birds you may shoot the partridge or the loon, the eagle or the duck . . . [until recently] this region was not often visited by summer tourists. A trip to the Adirondacks was viewed as something attended by great danger and incredible hardship. But now every season brings a great throng of nature-loving people from our large towns and cities, to rough it in the rude shanty, to sleep under white

Camp Pine Knot, Raquette Lake, circa 1872. Raquette Lake was one place where city ways and fancy clothes were out of fashion. A swinging hammock replaced the stiff-backed parlor chair!

View upstream, circa 1865.

Stairway leading to Table Rock, 1872.
The Ausable Chasm outdid its closest
competitor, Watkins Glen, when it came to
the awesome rugged wonders of nature.
The two-mile-long chasm, formed by the
river, ran as deep as 200 feet in some
places. The river's width and flow varied:
from a boiling torrent of 10 feet to a placid
sheet 50 feet wide. The steep sides of the
canyon rose in an endless variety of
shapes, and the dark cedars above cast a
somber gloom on the water.

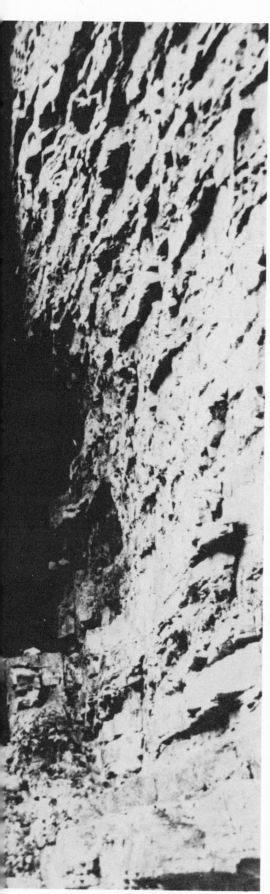

Ausable Chasm, view upstream, circa 1873.

tents that dot the wide expanse of living green, and to broil the appetizing venison steak, with their own hands, over the embers of the evening fire.''

Innumerable routes led into the northern wilderness. One popular route was from Port Kent on Lake Champlain, where visitors transferred to a four-horse stage for the ride at ten cents a head to Keeseville, across the Ausable River, and to Ausable House, where the traveler could anticipate a good supper and a comfortable night's rest. Only a mile from the hotel was the Ausable Chasm, a natural wonder that would "reward a voyage from Europe."

Otsego Lake, Cooperstown, circa 1872. Otsego Lake was considered one of the most picturesque in the state. A walk in the cemetery and a visit to Council Rock were two tips from the guidebooks on things to do. Long ago, the Indians had gathered to make their covenants at the round and bald Council Rock.

"No inland village in the Union probably excels Cooperstown in elegance of situation and beauty of surrounding scenery. Otsego Lake, in the immediate vicinity, is a most beautiful sheet of water, abounding in trout and bass, celebrated for their peculiar flavor." Cooperstown had once been the home of James Fenimore Cooper, America's popular storyteller. Scenes from several Leatherstocking Tales were drawn from the beautiful hilly lake region nearby.

By 1871 luxurious railroad cars replaced the "tedious lumbering" stages from Albany to Cooperstown, and the village had an excellent hotel—the Cooper House—and a half dozen smaller hotels and boardinghouses. Steamers made regular rounds of Otsego Lake every day, and a new three-hundred-passenger steamer, the *Natty Bumppo*, made its debut in the 1871 season. Sailboats and rowboats were always for hire, and a small steamer was available to charter. Local places of interest were within an easy walk from town—Hannah's Hill, West Hill, Prospect Rock, Council Rock, Cooper's old house and grave, Lakewood Cemetery, and Fairy Spring.

Visitors to Cooperstown often made side trips to see the celebrated Richfield Springs and Sharon Springs, and the lake steamer connected with a stage for either resort. Richfield Springs, with its healing waters, long known to the Indians, was on the grounds of the Spring House Hotel, though invalids who came seeking cures at the springs often stayed at good private houses away from the bustle of hotel life. The lake swarmed in summer with exuberant picnic and fishing parties. Hotels on the lakefront thoughtfully furnished their guests with boats, fishing tackle, and refreshments.

Next on the tourist's itinerary was Trenton Falls. By all reports, the hotel there was the best anywhere for comfort, cleanliness, and good food. A foreign visitor in 1833 wrote about his visit. After traversing the mountainous road to the hotel, he went immediately to view the falls, only two hundred yards away. Though he admired them, he did not care for the native way of doing things: "The Americans possess a most singular taste for marring the beauty of every place which can boast of anything like scenery, by introducing a bar-room into the most romantic and conspicuous spot. Consequently there is a little white, painted-wooden shanty perched upon the very brow of the High Fall, from which all kinds of liquors are distributed to the yankee admirers of nature, after they have undergone the overpowering fatigue of walking four hundred yards from the hotel."

Some years later, Nathaniel Willis wrote more kindly about the "shanty": "Here a flight of stairs, leads up to a house of refreshment styled the 'Rural Retreat,' twenty feet above the summit of the high falls . . . [It is] a house thirty by sixteen, with a well furnished bar, and also a room for gentlemen and ladies, encircled and shaded by hemlocks and cedars, from the front platform and windows of which is a full view of the inverted scenery of the falls, of the flat rock below, and of the

View from Carmichael Point, Trenton Falls, circa 1875. "Here the river has formed an immense excavation, and falls some forty feet into its bed below with a furious roaring." The eerie atmosphere and the sharp descent of the stairway led one visitor to remark that the wife who treads here needs to be on good terms with her husband, lest he push her in.

Glen Mountain House on North Cliff, Watkins Glen, circa 1871. "We reached the broad veranda of the Mountain House ... surrounded by a gay and excited company of visitors, all agog with what they have seen and what they expect to see .... One steps out to stretch his legs in the saloon, in the society of ice-creams, lemonades, simpering smiles and every-day affectations."

Sulphur Bath Houses, Sharon Springs, circa 1868. Many rheumatics came to Sharon Springs, some so feeble they had to be carried to the bathing house near the two famous springs—Magnesia and White Sulphur.

visitors who pass upon it to survey the exhibition above." It was said by others that the portico of the building "trembles like an autumn leaf" from the roar of the cataract.

If the tourist was in the mood for waterfalls, a visit to Ithaca at the head of Lake Cayuga would satisfy his desire, for the area had fifteen waterfalls, some very beautiful. And from the town of Cayuga the visitor could proceed to Taghkanic Falls—fifty feet higher than Niagara —then go on to Geneva and Seneca Lake. Steamboats ran daily from Geneva to Watkins Glen, one of the biggest tourist attractions in the country. Secretary Seward, seeking to show off a bit of America, once brought the entire diplomatic corps for a tour of the Glen. In 1870, according to hotel registers, over sixty thousand people visited the area.

The entrance to Watkins Glen was a short walk from town. A series of strongly braced stairways led upward into the gorge to the majestic

Portage Railroad Bridge, Portage, New York, circa 1872. The Erie Railroad's bridge over the Genesee Falls, at Portage, was called the largest wooden bridge in the world. It burned on May 6, 1875.

Watkins Glen, circa 1880. A typical vacationer with children beside the covered bridge.

beauty beyond. "First, we come to Glen Alpha, where the river pours and swirls in cascades through the great chasm, and dashes its spray high up on the steep walls. The place grows more and more weird, and we seem to be amid the ruins of some wonderful primitive world. The rocks take on the most grotesque forms, and the abyss, along whose sides we clamber on the rude stairway, sends up a cold chill like that from a charnel-house. The walls above our heads rise tier on tier to a height which shuts out all but a narrow strip of the blue sky." Then the footpath led out of the gloom into bright sunlight. The cheerful veranda of the Mountain House, perched on a ledge, was a welcome sight. The hotel served ice creams and delectable lemonades to a constant stream of busy tourists.

The traveler's next train stop westward was just south of Rochester, at Avon Village, home of the well-known Avon Springs, whose waters were not only taken internally but also used for bathing. Some called the sprightly resort a perpetual picnic, with its busy hotels and comfortable boardinghouses. When it was drinking time at the Lower Spring, omnibuses and carriages brought in crowds of people from the village to sip the curative waters. "Grimace was the prevailing feature of countenance when swallowing the beverage for the first few days, and grotesque groups were thus often formed around the fountain."

At this point in his journey, the tourist had several choices—Chautauqua Lake, in the extreme western corner of the state—Niagara Falls, the dream of all vacationers—or he could head northward for the fabled Thousand Islands.

Genesee Valley and Lake View, circa 1878. Small hotels and boardinghouses were the rule in the lake country, lending themselves to the gentle pursuits of croquet, telescope viewing, or just idling about in the mild weather.

Niagara Falls

A knowing Yankee said Niagara Falls was the "most bridy" place he knew. It was a bit scandalous to British visitors in 1869 to see so much hugging and kissing on the stairs of the Cataract House, the most patronized hotel on the American side of the falls. The hotel seemed to be the "rendezvous of all the newly-married couples of New England."

The American side of the falls appeared to be the most popular with the "Niagara mad" English visitors, at least for sleeping. The lonely forest of the turn of the century had given way by the 1830s to hotels, outbuildings, gardens, and small establishments. Also making their appearance were mills, museums, staircases, grogshops, and the inevitable tolls to points of interest. Bridges had been strung from island to island to get a better view of the falls.

Some visitors said the view was better from the Canadian side. A "garish hotel" (according to an English visitor) was not far from the Canadian Horseshoe Falls and a magnificent view of Niagara Falls could be seen from Table Rock, a large, projecting slab nor far from the inn. A Mr. Coke, of the British army, visited the falls in August 1832 and wrote of his experiences. He said two guides who lived near Table Rock had each built a spiral staircase downward along its sides to the rocky base eighty to ninety feet below. Along the bank was a path that led to a cave under the Horseshoe Falls. Before making the fearful excursion on a stormy day, Mr. Coke and two companions had to take off their clothes and dress in uncomfortable oilskin garments and a glazed hat provided by the guides. The shoes, also provided, had "evidently visited the water daily for two or three years." They then descended the steep staircases. Soon they were on a narrow ledge that led into a fifty-foot-long cavern and were greeted by a dense cloud of spray. Mr. Coke boldly told the guide to lead on through the thick, dark mist. "The path was at first a narrow ledge of rock, only a few inches in breadth, and affording but a very insecure footing; the guide however grasped one of my hands firmly, while with the other I took hold of the

The Honeymoon, circa 1885. "Do not seek for occasion to tease him .... Do not lead him about as if in triumph: nor take advantage of the ascendancy which you have gained by playing with his feelings." Advice to the newlyweds–Decorum, 1881.

View below Table Rock, 1837. For years daring visitors, sometimes as many as fifty, stood out on the ledge of rock despite the warning that large sections had fallen into the river below. Guides often fired pistol shots before venturing out onto the ledge. A large crack appeared in 1867 and the Canadians blasted the remaining portion, leaving but a huge pile of rocks at the river's edge below.

rough projections of rock. The wind, which equalled a tornado, blew the water against my face in such torrents that I could hardly see." When Termination Rock was reached, the storm dashed water on the visitor's face so that he could see nothing. He amused himself by shouting into the deafening roar as his guide gathered a quantity of eels from the loose stones. Several days later, on a clear day, he returned with his friends and saw that the "vast curved sheet over head now looked beautifully white and glaring, presenting an effect similar to that of the sun's rays upon ground glass."

Both the Canadians and Americans experimented with the violent power of the great falls. Three large British ships, used in the War of 1812 and stationed at Lake Erie, were condemned, and it was decided to send them over the falls to see the amount of destruction caused. The first boat was torn apart by the rapids before going over and the second filled with water before it reached the falls, but the third "took the leap gallantly, and retained her form till lost in the cloud of mist below." Only a fragment of it a foot long was later found. In 1827 it was the Americans' turn to try a ship over the falls. Two bears, a deer, a buffalo, and several small animals were on board. The rapids tore the ship up quite a bit, but a large part of the hull went over. One account said she drew eighteen feet of water but did not strike the cliff when she took the plunge. Accounts of the story differ, one claiming that the two bears swam to safety before the boat was dashed to pieces on the rocks below.

In June 1829, a haggard young man, Francis Abbot, carrying a large portfolio, several books, and musical instruments, first made his appearance at the Village of the Falls, on the American side. After a few weeks of sightseeing, he fell in love with the place and took up residence in a ramshackle old cottage on Goat Island. He made day and night appearances walking about the islands and bathing in the rapids and became known as the hermit of the falls. One day in June 1831 he bathed once too often in the rushing river. His clothes were found on the bank and ten days later his body was discovered and brought back for burial near the falls.

After the railroad came to Buffalo, it was easy to reach Niagara Falls, only an hour away. More and more people came from home and abroad to see the great natural wonder, and it became a fashionable resort for summer and fall. George William Curtis, writing of his trip in 1851, said that before the train stopped at the station, a crowd of men leaped from the cars and ran, not with enthusiasm to see the falls, but to get first choice of rooms at the Cataract House, situated so that the rapids above the American falls could be seen to great advantage. The first thing a visitor usually did after registering was to hire a hack to take him to the suspension bridge built in 1855, about two miles below the falls. The bridge was a marvel of engineering, with a lower level for

General view of Niagara Falls, circa 1897. For almost a century, guidebooks had warned their readers to beware of the prices charged tourists at Niagara Falls. Still the people kept coming – in greater numbers every year.

177

Elevator Tower, Suspension Bridge, circa 1875. A second suspension bridge was built across Niagara River, near the American Falls, in 1869. The bridge was blown down during a storm in 1889, and six years later an all-steel suspension bridge was erected.

Roebling Suspension Bridge from its tower, circa 1868. Bridges kept coming and going over Niagara River. Aside from their more practical uses, they were the perfect spots for viewing the wonders of Niagara Falls.

Maid of the Mist, circa 1877. About three miles below the falls was a frightfully wild spot called the Whirlpool, where tourists shuddered as they watched trees, dead animals, and other debris carried round and round into the eddy. In 1861 the Maid of the Mist *tried to escape her American creditors during a slow tourist season by running through the Whirlpool and rapids to the Canadian side—a run no boat could survive. "She plunged through the rolling white caps with a rush but lost her smokestack as huge waves swept her deck."*

carriages and an upper one for trains, and tourists were always eager to climb to the upper one to view the scene. Just above the bridge, on the American side, a road wound down the bank until "it reached the water's edge in a little bend; and here is the lower landing of the *Maid of the Mist*—a little steamer seen just now stemming the torrent as she creeps along the shore on her voyage to the Falls . . . her oilcloth passengers look like pigmies."

The easy way to take the trip on the *Maid of the Mist* was to meet the boat at the landing near the fall. "The descent on the American side is facilitated by an inclined plane, on which is a double track, so that one car ascends as the other descends. The cars are moved by a water-wheel which is turned by a branch of the cataract itself. By the side of the railway is a flight of stairs—over seven hundred in number. We soon reached the *Maid of the Mist*—moored by the wharf. The

"Signorina Maria Spelterini Crossing Whirlpool Rapids, Niagara, on a Rope." In 1876 thousands lined Roebling's old bridge, top and bottom, to watch Maria Spelterini, the pretty Italian acrobat, cross the falls on a wire backwards, with weighted bags attached to her feet.

"The Landing," circa 1838. Mr. Gadsby, world traveler, English to the core, visited Niagara falls in 1873. Expectations had led him to believe the falls would be 500 feet high, and he was disappointed to find them a mere 160 feet. Yet the breadth, the roar and splash, and the dashing up of foam and spray made him admit—"It was one of the grandest sights I had ever beheld."

"A tender moment," circa 1890.

gentlemanly captain approaches, furnishes our oil-cloth suits—enveloping the head as well as the body . . . we glide up near the bottom of the American fall, pass along the foot of Iris Island, and curve around near the great horse-shoe fall. There is no view of the fall more grand or impressive than that obtained in this passage."

When visitors returned to Cataract House for dinner, they were treated to a list of the new arrivals on the backs of their bills of fare. Notables from all over the world stopped at the hotel, and "misspelled" names on the menu caused a great deal of merriment. British visitors found especially to their liking the several strong current baths in the hotel. A small stream of water was diverted from the rapids opposite the hotel and led through a hole in the wall into two deep tubs resembling large troughs. The current came through with a great rush and made a refreshing treat, especially in hot weather.

Genuine acrobats and travelling fakirs of all sorts invariably showed up at the falls to gain their measure of notoriety. Politicians and literary critics were having some twinges in the 1880s about the cheap vulgarity surrounding America's great attraction. "Niagara is made a huge circus show, surrounded by every kind of pretty degradation." By 1898 open trolley cars ran on each side of the river to all points of interest. But if Niagara had lost its charm as a fashionable resort it still attracted short-stay visitors and love-struck honeymooners who thrilled to the falls and saw none of the tawdriness of commercialism but only the beauty of the scene.

179

The Thousand Islands

For the sporting crowd no resort could compare with the Thousand Islands on the St. Lawrence River. "During the months of July and August, pleasure parties from the surrounding country, and strangers from a distance, resórt here for their amusement, enjoying themselves to their heart's content by hunting, fishing, bathing, being surrounded by wild and interesting scenery and invigorating air, not exceeded by any section of the United States or Canada."

The St. Lawrence flowing in from Lake Ontario becomes in the course of a few miles so wide and so full of islands that it was called The Lake of the Thousand Islands. No fewer than three thousand fairyland islands of every imaginable size and shape dot the area, some tiny, others covering acres. Some are bare masses of rock, others are thickly wooded.

Hunters and fishermen had long known the islands, but the area did not develop as a resort until 1846 when the first Crossmon House was built, in Alexandria Bay, to accommodate ten guests. The venture proved so popular that the owners enlarged the building several times: in 1850 for thirty guests, 1864 for seventy-five, and finally in 1873 for three hundred. The list of visitors to the hotel held some distinguished names, including Martin Van Buren and his son.

The resort-building boom, at its zenith during the seventies, caught on in the Thousand Islands. The small islands were going at bargain prices and were snapped up for summer home sites. The new houses ranged from fishing shacks to comfortable and expensive homes with architecture ranging from gingerbread to chateau styles.

In 1873 a huge new hotel called the Thousand Island House opened. An instant success, every room in this well-appointed hotel remained full during the season. Guests had the exclusive use of a mineral spring on the hotel grounds.

The Methodists established a community called Thousand Island Park on the southern tip of Wells Island, a popular spot for recreation

View of the Thousand Island House, from the veranda of the Crossman House, Alexandria Bay, circa 1875. "And its immediate surroundings will ever be the grand central point of interest to all who turn their steps northward in search of the pleasures of the sportsman, or the rest and recreation needed by all workers."

Balloon ascension at the Thousand Island House, on July 24, 1873. Mr. I. A. Squires, of Utica, is about to make an ascent before an admiring crowd.

Museum, Thousand Island Park, circa 1878, opposite. The Methodist meetings— religious, scientific, and literary in character—were held in Thousand Island Park, on one end of Wells Island. The resort had been subdivided into broad grass-covered avenues with cottages and tents nesting between the trees and foliage. "All for all, it is by far the most pleasant of all parks devoted to such purposes," said its minister and manager of the park, who saw to it that rental tents could be had at reasonable rates.

Lawn party, Hamilton, Ontario, circa 1877.

Fishing party at Frost's Island, circa 1875.

Mussey Family after dining, circa 1873.

and camp meetings, with a good dock and a number of private homes.

Good and easy transportation by rail and boat brought throngs of visitors to the Lake of a Thousand Islands. "The air is light, dry and mellow, and is adapted to the constitution of almost every one, producing a kind of peace-with-all-the-world feeling and endowing one with a new and wondrous activity. To the new comer of this Paradise of America, the noble St. Lawrence seems not at all like a river, but rather like a great lake, spreading out to miles in breadth . . . most of which, especially in the vicinity of the Thousand Island House, is thickly studded with the most enchanting islands, wooded and cleared."

The Rapids, St. Lawrence River, circa 1882. One of the greatest thrills was a steamboat excursion along the rapids of the St. Lawrence from Ogdensburg to Montreal. It was reported that on entering the rapids, the engineer shut off the motor and a pilot guided the steamboat between reefs and breakwater at sixty miles an hour! One visitor, in 1856, recalled that an Indian pilot named Baptiste was brought aboard to steer the boat through the last and most dangerous rapid, Lachine. It was said that no other man could pilot a steamer across these rapids.

President Chester Alan Arthur goes fishing in the Thousand Islands. Mathew Brady, the famous Civil War photographer, traveled with President Arthur to make a pictorial record of the President's Thousand Island vacation.

President Arthur embarks for fishing, 1882. Fishing parties sometimes hired a steam yacht to tow them in their small boats. A shrill whistle from the yacht called in the little boats at the dinner hour for a bill of fare featuring the freshly caught fish.

President Arthur on an afternoon picnic, 1882.

President Arthur in front of the Crossman House, 1882.

President Arthur netting his catch, 1882.

𝓑ibliography

ALEXANDER, ROBERT CROZER. *Ho! For Cape Island!* Published by the author. Cape May, New Jersey: 1956.

Appleton's General Guide to the United States and Canada. Part 1. New England and Middle States and Canada. New York: D. Appleton, 1888.

Appleton's Hand-Book of American Travel—Northern and Eastern Tours. New York: D. Appleton, 1876.

Appleton's Hand-Book Through the United States. New York: D. Appleton, 1846.

Asbury Park Journal. 1878.

Atlantic Coast Guide, The. New York: E. P. Dutton and Company, 1873.

BACHELDER, JOHN B. *Bachelder's Illustrated Tourist Guide of the United States.* Boston: 1873, 1875.

BARBER, JOHN W., and HOWE, HENRY. *Historical Collections of the State of New Jersey.* New York: 1844.

————. *Historical Collections . . . of every town in Massachusetts . . .* Worcester: Door, Howland & Company, 1839.

BEARSE, RAY, ed. *Vermont: A Guide to the Green Mountain State.* Boston: Houghton Mifflin Company, 1966.

BEEBE, LUCIUS. *Mr. Pullman's Elegant Palace Car.* New York: Doubleday and Company, Inc., 1961.

Book of Cape May, New Jersey, A. Cape May: Albert Hand Company, 1937.

BRAIDER, DONALD. *The Niagara.* New York: Holt, Rinehart and Winston, 1972.

BROWNELL, W. C. *Newport.* New York: Charles Scribner's Sons, 1894.

BUEL, J. W. *America's Wonderlands.* Boston: J. S. Round, 1893.

BUTLER, FRANK. *Butler's Book of the Boardwalk.* Atlantic City: 1952.

Canadian Handbook and Tourist's Guide . . . Montreal: M. Longmoore and Company, 1867.

Cape May Gazette. 1886.

Clarendon House. A brochure. Rutland: Tuttle and Co., 1876.

CLUNE, HENRY W. *The Genesee.* New York: Holt, Rinehart, and Winston, 1963.

COKE, EDWARD THOMAS. *A Subaltern's Furlough.* 2 Vols. New York: J. & J. Harper, 1833.

COLT, MRS. S. S. *The Tourist's Guide: Through the Empire State . . . By Hudson River and New York Central Route.* Published by the author. Albany, New York: 1871.

COOK, JOEL. *Brief Summer Rambles near Philadelphia.* Philadelphia: J. B. Lippincott & Company, 1882.

Cornhill Magazine, The. 1894.

Cosmopolitan, The. 1892.

Crab, The. 1881.

CURTIS, GEORGE WILLIAM. *Lotus-Eating.* New York: Harper & Brothers, 1852.

DANIELS, MORRIS S. *The Story of Ocean Grove.* Cincinnati: The Methodist Book Concern, 1919.

DARRAH, WILLIAM CULP. *Stereo Views.* Gettysburg: Times and News Publishing Company, 1964.

DEARBORN, R. F. *Saratoga and How to See It . . .* Saratoga: C. D. Slocum, 1872.

DEARBORN, R. F. *Saratoga Illustrated . . .* Troy: 1872.

Decorum. A Practical Treatise on Etiquette and Dress of the Best American Society. New York: Union Publishing House, 1881.

DE COSTA, B. F. *Lake George; its Scenes and Characteristics.* New York: Anson D. F. Randolph and Company, 1869.

DE LISSER, R. LIONEL. *Picturesque Catskills; Green County.* Northampton: 1894. Reprint with foreword by Alf Evers. Cornwallville: 1971.

DICEY, EDWARD. *Six Months in the Federal States.* 2 Vols. London & Cambridge: Macmillan & Company, 1863.

DISTURNELL, J. *The Traveler's Guide to the Hudson River, Saratoga Springs, Lake George . . .* New York: American News Company, 1864.

————. *Springs, Water-Falls, Sea-Bathing Resorts, and Mountain Scenery of the United States and Canada . . . Mineral Springs . . . Fashionable Watering Places . . .* New York: J. Disturnell, 1855.

DIX, JOHN ROSS. *A Hand-Book of Newport, and Rhode Island.* Newport: C. E. Hammett, Jr., 1852.

DWIGHT, THEODORE. *Summer Tours or, Notes of a Traveler Through Some of the Middle and Northern States.* New York: Harper & Brothers, 1847.

Eaglewood Press. 1862.

ELWELL, EDWARD. *Portland and Vicinity.* Revised and edited by Robert Grieve. Portland: 1887.

EVERS, ALF. *The Catskills: From Wilderness to Woodstock.* New York: Doubleday, 1972.

FAITHFULL, MISS EMILY. *Three Visits to America.* New York: Fowler & Wells

Steamer in Dick's Bay, Thousand Islands, circa 1873. Photographer Anthony in foreground.

Company, 1884.

FERRIS, GEORGE T., ed. *Our Native Land*. New York: D. Appleton and Company, 1882.

GADSBY, JOHN. *A Visit to Canada and the United States of America* ... London: Gadsby, 1873.

Gladness of the Sea. Nineteenth Annual Report of the President of the Ocean Grove Camp-Meeting Association of the Methodist Episcopal Church, 1888.

Godey's Lady's Book. 1849, 1865, 1875.

Graham's Magazine. 1847, 1850.

GRANT, ROBERT. *The North Shore of Massachusetts*. New York: Charles Scribner's Sons, 1896.

Great Industries of the United States. Hartford: J. B. Burr & Hyde, 1872.

Guide Book to Mohonk Lake. New York: Chas M. Green Printing Company, 1883.

HALL, JOHN F. *The Daily Union History of Atlantic City and County*. Atlantic City: The Daily Union Printing Company, 1900.

Harper's Monthly Magazine. 1850–81.

HAYWARD, JOHN. *The New England Gazetteer; Containing Descriptions of all the States, Counties and Towns in New England*. Concord: Israel S. Boyd & William White, 1839.

HILL, RALPH NADING. *Yankee Kingdom*. New York: Harper and Row, 1960.

HINE, C. G. *The Story of Martha's Vineyard*. New York: Hine Brothers, 1908.

History of Ocean Grove, New Jersey Diamond Jubilee 1869–1944. Ocean Grove Camp Meeting Association, 1944.

Holden's Magazine. 1851.

Knickerbocker New York Monthly Magazine. 1839.

KOBBÉ, GUSTAV. *The New Jersey Coast and Pines*. Short Hills: 1889.

Ladies' Repository. 1856.

Lady's Friend, The. 1868.

LAIGHTON, OSCAR. *Ninety Years at the Isles of Shoals*. Andover: 1929.

LATROBE, CHARLES JOSEPH. *The Rambler in North America: 1832–1833*. Second edition. 2 Vols. London: Seeley, Fleet St., 1836. Reprinted by Johnson Reprint Corp., New York, 1970.

LESLIE, MRS. FRANK. *California a Pleasure Trip from Gotham to the Golden Gate*. New York: G. W. Carelton & Co., 1877.

LYELL, CHARLES, ESQ. F. R. S. *Travels in North America in the Years 1841–42*. 2 Vols. New York: Wiley and Putnam, 1845.

Mc Clure's Magazine. 1895.

MC CULLOUGH, EDO. *Good Old Coney Island*. New York: Charles Scribner's Sons, 1957.

Maine Historical Society Newsletter, Vol. 10, No. 4 (May 1871).

MARSHALL, W. G., M. A. *Through America; or Nine Months in the United States*. London: Sampson Low, Marston, Searle, Rivington, 1881.

MAYHEW, ELEANOR R., ed. *Martha's Vineyard*. Edgartown: Dukes County Historical Society, Inc., 1956.

MERRILL, ARCH. *The Lakes Country*. Reprinted from *The Democrat and Chronicle*. Rochester: Louis Heindl & Son, 1944.

Monmouth Democrat. 1879.

MOORMAN, J. J. *The Mineral Waters of the United States and Canada*. Baltimore: Kelly & Piet, 1867.

MOSS, GEORGE H., JR. *Double Exposure: Early Stereographic Views of Historic Monmouth County, New Jersey and Their Relationship to Pioneer Photography*. Sea Bright: Ploughshare Press, 1971.

Munsey's Magazine. 1896, 1897.

New-Mirror, The. New York: 1844.

New-York Mirror and Ladies Literary Gazette, The. 1827.

NORTON, CHARLES L., ed. *American Seaside Resorts; A Hand-Book For Health and Pleasure Seekers*. New York: Taintor Bros., 1871.

Ocean Beach. 1879.

Ocean Grove Camp Meeting Report, 1877, 1878.

Our Summer Retreats; A Hand-Book to all the Chief Waterfalls, Springs, Mountains and Sea-side Resorts ... *in the United States*. New York: T. Nelson and Sons, 1858.

PERKINS, ELI. *Saratoga 1901*. New York: Sheldon and Company, 1872.

Putnam's Monthly Magazine. 1853, 1854.

Red Bank Register. 1886.

Reminiscenses of America in 1869. By Two Englishmen. London: Low, Son, and Marston, 1870.

ROCKLAND, MICHAEL AARON, trans. *Sarmiento's Travels in the United States in 1847*. Princeton: Princeton University Press, 1970.

Salter's History of Monmouth and Ocean Counties, New Jersey. Bayonne: 1890.

SARGENT, WILLIAM M. *An Historical Sketch, Guide Book, and Prospectus of Cushing's Island*. New York: 1886.

Scribner's Monthly Magazine. 1873-94.

Shore Press, The. 1881.

SMITH, J. CALVIN. *The Illustrated Hand-Book, a New Guide for Travelers* ... New York: Sherman Smith, 1846.

STAPLES, O. G. *The Thousand Island House*. A brochure. 1881.

State of New York: Embracing Historical, Descriptive, and Statistical Notices ... *County Towns, Lakes, Rivers, Railroads, etc.* Compiled and edited by Henry Kollock. New York: Henry Kollock, 1883.

STEVENS, LEWIS TOWNSEND. *The History of Cape May County, New Jersey from the Aboriginal Times to the Present Day* ... Cape May: Lewis T. Stevens, 1897.

STODDARD, S. R. *Lake George; A Book of To-Day*. Albany: Weed, Parsons and Company, 1873.

STONE, WILLIAM L. *Reminiscences of Saratoga and Ballston*. New York: R. Worthington, 1880.

Summer Excursion Routes. Published by Pennsylvania Railroad Company, 1898.

SWEETSER, MOSES FORSTER. *Summer Days Down East*. Portland: Chisholm Brothers, 1883.

———. *Views in the White Mountains*. Portland: Chisholm Brothers, 1879.

Torch, The. Asbury Park: 1889.

TUCKERMAN, HENRY T. *America and Her Commentators*. New York: Charles Scribner, 1864.

ULYAT, WILLIAM C. *Life at the Sea Shore*. Princeton: Ginness Runyan, 1880.

VINCENT, REV. H. *A History of the Wesleyan Grove, Martha's Vineyard Camp Meeting*. Boston: George C. Rand & Avery, 1858.

Source Notes for Photographers

The following is a list of types of the original photographs, names of photographers and photographic firms, and names of printers and publishers of the photographs reproduced in this book, when they are known. Listings correspond to pictures as they appear from left to right.

Key to Abbreviations

Style or type of original photograph

A_____Ambrotype   E_____Engraving or lithograph   S_____Paper print, double (stereograph)
C_____Collotype   P_____Paper print, single   T_____Tintype (ferrotype)

Page	Type	Photographer/Artist	Publisher/Printer	Page	Type	Photographer/Artist	Publisher/Printer
2	S	S. R. Stoddard Glens Falls, N.Y.	Stoddard Glens Falls, N.Y.	30–31	P	Unknown	Unknown
6	T	Unknown	Unknown	32	S	Unknown	Unknown
9	P	Unknown	Unknown	33	P	Unknown	Unknown
10	S	Unknown	Unknown	34–35	S	O. H. Willard Philadelphia, Pa.	Willard Philadelphia, Pa.
10	P	Unknown	Unknown	35	S	O. H. Willard Philadelphia, Pa.	Willard Philadelphia, Pa.
11	S	Unknown	Unknown	36	P	Unknown	Unknown
12	E		J. H. Lutz Old Orchard, Me.	36	P	Unknown	Unknown
				37	P	Unknown	Unknown
12	S	Unknown	C. H. Graves Philadelphia, Pa.	38	S	O. H. Willard Philadelphia, Pa.	Willard Philadelphia, Pa.
13	S	B. W. Kilburn Littleton, N.H.	J. M. Davis Littleton, N.H.	39	S	W. H. Rau Washington, D.C.	Griffith & Griffith Philadelphia, Pa.
13	S	Unknown	Underwood & Underwood New York, N.Y.	39	S	O. H. Willard Philadelphia, Pa.	Willard Philadelphia, Pa.
13	S	W. H. Rau Washington, D.C.	Griffin & Griffin Philadelphia, Pa.	40	S	Harry Phillips Philadelphia, Pa.	Phillips Philadelphia, Pa.
14–15	P	Byron New York, N.Y.	Byron New York, N.Y.	41	T	Unknown	Unknown
16	S	L. E. Walker Warsaw, N.Y.	Walker Warsaw, N.Y.	42	S	W. M. Chase Baltimore, Md.	Chase Baltimore, Md.
17	S	Strohmeyer & Wyman New York, N.Y.	Underwood & Underwood New York, N.Y.	42–43	S	J. F. Jarvis Washington, D.C.	Underwood & Underwood New York, N.Y.
17	P	Lewis Alman Lake Mahopac, N.Y.	Alman Lake Mahopac, N.Y.	43	S	Unknown	Unknown
				44	S	A. J. Fisher New York, N.Y.	Fisher New York, N.Y.
17	T	Unknown	Unknown	45	S	W. H. Rau Washington, D.C.	Underwood & Underwood New York, N.Y.
18	S	Delos Barnum Cortland, N.Y.	Barnum Cortland, N.Y.	46	S	B. W. Kilburn Littleton, N.H.	Kilburn Bros. Littleton, N.H.
20	S	Unknown	H. Rope's & Co. New York, N.Y.	47	S	B. W. Kilburn Littleton, N.H.	Kilburn Bros. Littleton, N.H.
20	S	B. W. Kilburn Littleton, N.H.	Kilburn Bros. Littleton, N.H.	48	T	Unknown	Unknown
20	E		Unknown	49	P	Stafford Asbury Park, N.J.	Stafford Asbury Park, N.J.
20	E		Unknown				
22	S	B. W. Kilburn Littleton, N.H.	Kilburn Bros. Littleton, N.H.	50–51	S	Pach Bros. New York, N.Y.	Pach Bros. New York, N.Y.
23	S	Unknown	E. & H. T. Anthony New York, N.Y.	52	S	G. W. Pach New York, N.Y., & Long Branch, N.J.	Pach Bros. New York, N.Y., & Long Branch, N.J.
24	S	G. W. Pach New York, N.Y., & Long Branch, N.J.	Pach Bros. New York, N.Y., & Long Branch, N.J.	53	S	G. W. Pach New York, N.Y., & Long Branch, N.J.	Pach Bros. New York, N.Y., & Long Branch, N.J.
24	S	Baker & Record Saratoga, N.Y.	Baker & Record Saratoga, N.Y.	55	S	G. W. Pach New York, N.Y., & Long Branch, N.J.	Pach Bros. New York, N.Y., & Long Branch, N.J.
25	S	Unknown	Littleton View Co. Littleton, N.H.				
25	S	Unknown	Underwood & Underwood New York, N.Y.	56	S	G. W. Pach New York, N.Y., & Long Branch, N.J.	Pach Bros New York, N.Y., & Long Branch, N.J.
26	S	S. H. Morris Auburn, N.Y.	Morris Auburn, N.Y.	57	T	Unknown	Unknown
27	S	Clough & Kimball Concord, N.H.	Clough & Kimball Concord, N.H.	58	S	G. W. Pach New York, N.Y., & Long Branch, N.J.	Pach Bros. New York, N.Y., & Long Branch, N.J.
27	S	F. A. Morrill New Sharon, Me.	Morrill New Sharon, Me.	58	S	G. W. Pach New York, N.Y., & Long Branch, N.J.	Pach Bros. New York, N.Y., & Long Branch, N.J.
28–29	S	S. H. Morris Auburn, N.Y.	Morris Auburn, N.Y.				

Page	Type	Photographer/Artist	Publisher/Printer
59	S	G. W. Pach New York, N.Y., & Long Branch, N.J.	Pach Bros. New York, N.Y., & Long Branch, N.J.
60	S	Unknown	Unknown
60	S	G. W. Pach New York, N.Y., & Long Branch, N.J.	Pach Bros. New York, N.Y., & Long Branch, N.J.
61	S	G. W. Pach New York, N.Y., & Long Branch, N.J.	Pach Bros. New York, N.Y., & Long Branch, N.J.
61	E	Woodcut	*Harper's Weekly,* August 14, 1869
62	S	C. Lane Red Bank, N.J.	New Jersey Stereo Co. Red Bank, N.J.
63	S	C. Lane Red Bank, N.J.	New Jersey Stereo Co. Red Bank, N.J.
63	S	G. W. Pach New York, N.Y., & Long Branch, N.J.	Pach Bros. New York, N.Y., & Long Branch, N.J.
64–65	P	Julius Wendt Albany, N.Y.	Wendt Albany, N.Y.
66	P	Byron New York, N.Y.	Byron New York, N.Y.
66	S	Unknown	London Stereoscopic Co.
67	P	Byron New York, N.Y.	Byron New York, N.Y.
67	P	Byron New York, N.Y.	Byron New York, N.Y.
67	P	Byron New York, N.Y.	Byron New York, N.Y.
68	E	Lithograph	Currier & Ives New York, N.Y.
69	S	Unknown	American Stereoptican Co. New York, N.Y.
70	P	Byron New York, N.Y.	Byron New York, N.Y.
72	S	Unknown	*American Scenery* New York, N.Y.
72	S	Unknown	Stereoscopic Gems of Coney Island
73	T	Unknown	Unknown
74	S	Unknown	Underwood & Underwood New York, N.Y.
74–75	P	E.W.N.	Unknown
75	P	Byron New York, N.Y.	Byron New York, N.Y.
75	P	Byron New York, N.Y.	Byron New York, N. Y.
76	S	Strohmeyer & Wyman New York, N.Y.	Underwood & Underwood New York, N.Y.
76	S	A. S. Campbell Elizabeth, N.J.	Campbell Elizabeth, N.J.
77	S	Unknown	Unknown
77	S	A. S. Campbell Elizabeth, N.J.	Campbell Elizabeth, N.J.
78	P	Unknown	Unknown
78–79	P	Unknown	Unknown
80	S	Unknown	Unknown
81	P	Unknown	Unknown
82	S	Reed's Rooms Newburyport, Mass.	Reed's Rooms Newburyport, Mass.
83	P	Unknown	Unknown
84	S	H. Q. Morton Providence, R.I.	Morton Providence, R.I.
84	S	Unknown	Unknown
85	S	Unknown	Hacker Photography Co. Providence, R.I.
86–87	P	Unknown	Unknown
88	P	G. D. Dunn Nevada, Ohio	Dunn Nevada, Ohio
89	S	Unknown	E & H. T. Anthony New York, N.Y.
89	S	J. P. Soule Boston, Mass.	American Views (Soule) Boston, Mass.
89	S	Unknown	Unknown
90	S	B. W. Kilburn Littleton, N.H.	Kilburn Littleton, N.H.
90	S	J. A. Williams Newport, R.I.	Williams Newport, R.I.
90	S	Unknown	E. & H. T. Anthony New York, N.Y.
91	P	Unknown	Unknown
91	S	Unknown	Unknown
92–93	P	Unknown	Unknown
92–93	P	Unknown	Unknown
93	E		*Our Native Land,* 1891
94	S	Woodward & Sons Taunton, Mass.	Woodward & Sons Taunton, Mass.
95	S	Unknown	Unknown
96	S	C. H. Shute & Sons Edgartown, Mass.	Shute & Sons Edgartown, Mass.
97	S	Unknown	Unknown
97	S	C. H. Shute & Sons Edgartown, Mass.	Shute & Sons Edgartown, Mass.
98	S	Brownell & Graham Fall River, Mass.	Brownell & Graham Fall River, Mass.
99	S	Brown & Gruban Fall River, Mass.	Brown & Gruban Fall River, Mass.
99	S	Unknown	Unknown
100	S	Unknown	Unknown
101	S	Unknown	Unknown
102	P	Unknown	Unknown
102	C	J. N. Chamberlain Woonsocket, R.I.	A. Witteman New York, N.Y.
104	S	Unknown	Unknown
105	S	C. Bullock Boston, Mass.	Bullock Boston, Mass.
106	S	Unknown	Gems of American Scenery
107	P	Unknown	Unknown
107	P	Unknown	Unknown
107	T	Unknown	Unknown
108	S	J. P. Soule Boston, Mass.	American Views (Soule) Boston, Mass.
109	S	J. H. Williams So. Scitiate, Mass.	Williams So. Scitiate, Mass.
109	S	G. K. Proctor Salem, Mass.	Proctor Salem, Mass.
110	S	J. S. Moulton Salem, Mass.	Moulton Salem, Mass.
111	S	C. B. Tuttle Lynn, Mass.	Tuttle Lynn, Mass.
112	S	Durgin, Gooding & Co. Old Orchard Beach, Me.	Durgin, Gooding & Co. Old Orchard Beach, Me.
112	P	Unknown	Unknown
113	T	Unknown	Unknown
114	T	Unknown	Unknown
114	S	Unknown	Unknown
115	P	Unknown	Unknown
116	E		Unknown
117	P	Unknown	Unknown
118	P	Unknown	Unknown
119	T	Unknown	Unknown
120–121	P	Unknown	Unknown
121	S	Unknown	Unknown
122	P	Unknown	Unknown
122	P	Unknown	Unknown
123	P	Unknown	Unknown
123	E	W. H. Bartlett London, England	*American Scenery* New York, N.Y.
124	P	Unknown	Unknown
125	P	Unknown	Unknown
127	P	Unknown	Unknown
128–129	S	C. H. Jennings Livonia, N.Y.	Jennings Livonia, N.Y.
130	P	Unknown	E & H. T. Anthony New York, N.Y.
131	T	Unknown	Unknown
132	S	Unknown	E & H. T. Anthony New York, N.Y.
132	S	J. Loeffler Staten Island, N.Y.	Loeffler Staten Island, N.Y.

Page	Type	Photographer/Artist	Publisher/Printer	Page	Type	Photographer/Artist	Publisher/Printer
132	S	J. W. & J. S. Moulton Salem, Mass.	Moulton Salem, Mass.	160	S	G. H. Hastings St. Johnsbury, Vt.	Hastings St. Johnsbury, Vt.
133	S	Unknown	E & H. T. Anthony New York, N.Y.	160	S	J. D. Heywood Boston, Mass.	F. Rowell Boston, Mass.
133	S	L.E. Walker Warsaw, N.Y.	Walker Warsaw, N.Y.	162	S	S. R. Stoddard Glens Falls, N.Y.	Stoddard Glens Falls, N.Y.
133	S	E. Lewis Kingston, N.Y.	Lewis Kingston, N.Y.	163	S	S. R. Stoddard Glens Falls, N.Y.	Stoddard Glens Falls, N.Y.
134–135	S	B. W. Kilburn Littleton, N.H.	Kilburn Bros. Littleton, N.H.	164	S	Unknown	Union View Co. Rochester, N.Y.
136	S	J. F. Soule Boston, Mass.	Soule Boston, Mass.	165	S	S. R. Stoddard Glens Falls, N.Y.	Stoddard Glens Falls, N.Y.
136	S	N. W. Pease No. Conway, N.H.	Pease No. Conway, N.H.	165	S	Unknown	Union View Co. Rochester, N.Y.
136	S	J. F. Soule Boston, Mass.	Soule Boston, Mass.	166	S	Unknown	Popular Series
137	S	J. F. Soule Boston, Mass.	Soule Boston, Mass.	166	P	Unknown	Unknown
137	S	B. W. Kilburn Littleton, N.H.	Kilburn Bros. Littleton, N.H.	167	S	S. R. Stoddard Glens Falls, N.Y.	Stoddard Glens Falls, N.Y.
137	S	Unknown	White Mountain Scenery	168	S	S. R. Stoddard Glens Falls, N.Y.	Stoddard Glens Falls, N.Y.
137	S	Unknown	E.J. Copp & Co.	168–169	S	H. S. Tousley Keeseville, N.Y.	Tousley Keeseville, N.Y.
138	C	Unknown	Chisholm Bros. Portland, Me.	169	S	H. K. Averill, Jr. Plattsburgh, N.Y.	Averill, Jr. Plattsburgh, N.Y.
139	S	Chapin & Penfield Albany, N.Y.	Chapin & Penfield Albany, N.Y.	170	S	Smith & Sayles Cooperstown, N.Y.	Smith & Sayles Cooperstown, N.Y.
139	S	B. W. Kilburn Littleton, N.H.	Kilburn Bros. Littleton, N.H.	170			
139	S	O. H. Cook Salem, Mass.	Cook Salem, Mass.	171	S	J. R. Moore Trenton Falls, N.Y.	Moore Trenton Falls, N.Y.
139	S	S. F. Adams New Bedford, Mass.	Adams New Bedford, Mass.	172	S	Unknown	Meske, Gilman & Rawson
140	S	S. F. Adams New Bedford, Mass.	Adams New Bedford, Mass.	172	S	G. F. Gates Watkins Glen, N.Y.	Gates Watkins Glen, N.Y.
140		Music cover: Parodi Kazurka	J.H. Searing & B. Brown	173	S	G. F. Gates Watkins Glen, N.Y.	Gates Watkins Glen, N.Y.
141	S	B. W. Kilburn Littleton, N.H.	Kilburn Bros. Littleton, N.H.	173	S	Unknown	Unknown
142–143	S	H. S. Fifield Lincoln, N.H.	Fifield Lincoln, N.H.	173	S	Betts Dansville, N.Y.	Betts Dansville, N.Y.
143	S	F. N. Granniss Waterbury, Conn.	Granniss Waterbury, Conn.	174	T	Unknown	Unknown
144	S	Baker & Record Saratoga, N.Y.	Baker & Record Saratoga, N.Y.	175	L	W. H. Bartlett London, England	*American Scenery* New York, N.Y.
145	P	Unknown	Unknown	176–177	S	Strohmeyer & Wyman New York, N.Y.	Underwood & Underwood New York, N.Y.
146	P	Unknown	Unknown	178	S	C. Bierstadt Niagara Falls, N.Y.	Bierstadt Niagara Falls, N.Y.
147	P	Unknown	Unknown	178	S	Unknown	Niagara Falls Series
147	P	Unknown	Unknown	178	S	C. Bierstadt Niagara Falls, N.Y.	Bierstadt Niagara Falls, N.Y.
148	P	Unknown	Unknown	179	L	W. H. Bartlett London, England	*American Scenery* New York, N.Y.
148	S	Baker & Record Saratoga, N.Y.	Baker & Record Saratoga, N.Y.	179	S	B. W. Kilburn Littleton, N.H.	J. M. Davis Littleton, N.H.
149	A	Unknown	Unknown	179	S	Unknown	Popular Series
149	S	B. W. Kilburn Littleton, N.H.	Kilburn Bros. Littleton, N.H.	180	S	W. Notman Montreal, Canada	Notman Montreal, Canada
150	P	N. Sarony New York, N.Y.	Sarony New York, N.Y.	180	S	A. C. McIntyre Alexandria Bay, N.Y.	McIntyre Alexandria Bay, N.Y.
151	E		*Leslie's*, August 14, 1875	181	S	A. C. McIntyre Alexandria Bay, N.Y.	McIntyre Alexandria Bay, N.Y.
152	E		*Godey's Lady's Book*, 1865	182	S	A. C. McIntyre Alexandria Bay, N.Y.	McIntyre Alexandria Bay, N.Y.
153	E		*Leslie's*, August 19, 1876	183	S	J. Esson Preston, Canada	Esson Preston, Canada
153	E		*Every Saturday,* September 9, 1871	183	S	A. C. McIntyre Alexandria Bay, N.Y.	McIntyre Alexandria Bay, N.Y.
154	P	Unknown	George S. Bolster Saratoga Springs, N.Y.	183	S	A.C. McIntyre Alexandria Bay, N.Y.	McIntyre Alexandria Bay, N.Y.
156	S	P. W. Taft Saxton's River, Vt.	Taft Saxton's River, Vt.	183	S	A. C. McIntyre Alexandria Bay, N.Y.	McIntyre Alexandria Bay, N.Y.
157	S	B. W. Kilburn Littleton, N.H.	Kilburn Bros. Littleton, N.H.	184	P	M. B. Brady Washington, D.C.	Brady Washington, D.C.
158	S	Unknown	Unknown	185	P	M. B. Brady Washington, D.C.	Brady Washington, D.C.
159	S	Unknown	Unknown	185	P	M. B. Brady Washington, D.C.	Brady Washington, D.C.
159	S	T. G. Richardson St. Albans, Vt.	Richardson St. Albans, Vt.	187	P	M. B. Brady Washington, D.C.	Brady Washington, D.C.
159	S	Unknown	Unknown				
160	S	J. D. Heywood Boston, Mass.	F. Rowell Boston, Mass.				

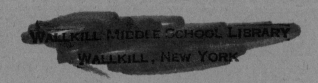